A Skills-based Approach t

Painting

is a Class Act

for

=

Years 3 and 4

Meg Fabian

Brilliant
PUBLICATIONS

We hope you and your pupils enjoy using the ideas in this book. Brilliant Publications publishes many other books for teaching art and design. To find out more details on any of the titles listed below, please log onto our website: www.brilliantpublications.co.uk.

Painting is a Class Act, Years 1–2	978-1-905780-29-7
Painting is a Class Act, Years 5–6	978-1-905780-31-0
Drawing is a Class Act, Years 1–2	978-1-903853-60-3
Drawing is a Class Act, Years 3–4	978-1-903853-61-0
Drawing is a Class Act, Years 5–6	978-1-903853-62-7
100+ Fun Ideas for Art Activities	978-1-905780-33-4
Preschool Art	978-1-897675-49-6
Discovering Great Artists	978-1-903853-16-0
The Big Messy Art Book	978-1-903853-18-4

Acknowledgements

I would like to thank the following primary schools for their permission to include in the publication examples of work by children in their schools. This work has been done over a number of years. Wherever work is named, permission was sought for inclusion.

Primary schools

Chawleigh Primary School
Filleigh Community Primary School

Clovelly Primary School
Witheridge C of E Primary School

Individual pupil list

Alfie Mathews
Andy Brown
Archie Muirhead
Beth Wilson
Bethany Peacock
Charlotte Hastie
Chris Nichols
Connie Ayres
Daisy Davies
Damian Hopkins
Daniel Huxtable
David Riley
David Young
Dominic Cork
Ebony Thorne
Eli Petch

Ellen Corrigan
Emily Sweet
Emma Parkhouse
Francis Huntingford
Harriet Gregory
Hannah Roberts
Hannah Stenning
Hayley Henry
Helen Elmer
Isabelle Kennedy-Brown
Ivy-May White
Jack Muirhead
Jasmine Hammet
Jay Latham
Jessica Hewit
Joe Blackford

Jordan Wild
Joshua Derbyshire
Karen Facey
Katya Toms
Laura Dennis
Luke Bray
Maddie Muirhead
Marie Roberts
Maya Barker
Morgan Johnson
Nicky Loat
Oliver Squire
Peter Rodgers
Polly Bray
Prince Sexon
Robert Steel

Roger Aggyman
Ruby Petch
Sam Warren
Shona Gregory
Shane Sexon
Steve Latham
Tabitha Waldron
Thomas Corras
Thomas Ellis
Thomas Parkhouse
Thomas Stodgel
Will Ayres
Wendy Stewart

Published by Brilliant Publications
Unit 10
Sparrow Hall Farm
Edlesborough
Dunstable
Bedfordshire
LU6 2ES, UK

Website: www.brilliantpublications.co.uk

General information enquiries:
Tel: 01525 222292

The name Brilliant Publications and the logo are registered trademarks.

Written by Meg Fabian
Designed by Bookcraft Limited
Front cover designed by Brilliant Publications

© Text Meg Fabian 2010
© Design Brilliant Publications 2010

Printed: ISBN 978-1-905780-30-3
eBook: ISBN 978-0-85747-126-0

First printed and published in the UK in 2010

Foreword

Being able to paint is a life-enhancing skill and the development of painting skills has benefits far beyond the art lesson. Painting:

* helps children to express themselves
* helps to promote high standards in other areas of the curriculum
* raises children's self-esteem and confidence
* gives children an understanding and awareness of colour which can be life enhancing.

This book will be invaluable to non-specialist teachers as it clearly:

* sets out the development of painting skills
* offers guidance on progression
* provides ideas to support classroom activities.

Meg Fabian is the ideal person to write this book. She is a specialist with a passion for art and has been instrumental in raising children's standards and confidence in art across a range of North Devon schools.

Phil Creek
Adviser for Art and Design
Devon Education Services

Contents

	Type of lesson	Time needed	Page
Basic skills			
Introducing powder paint			25
Investigating paintbrushes and making different brush strokes	Key Skill	1 hour	27
Making different brush strokes in a painting	Using Skill	30 min	28
Powder paint handling	Key Skill	30 min	29
Naming paint colours	Skill	20 min	30
Painting a picture in powder paint	Using Skill	1 hour	31
Getting to know the colours and comparing reds (or blues or yellows)	Using Skill	30 min	32
Making a colour lighter without using white (changing tone in colour)	Key Skill	20 min	33
Painting in one colour and making that colour lighter without using white (changing tone in colour)	Using Skill	30 min	34
Colour mixing			
Mixing colours			36
Mixing secondary colours: oranges (or greens or purples)	Key Skill	45 min	38
Mixing secondary colours	Using Skill	1 hour	39
Changing the colours by adding a little paint at a time	Skill	1 hour	40
Making a collage using work from the previous lesson	Activity	1 hour	41
Making a collage using work from the previous lesson (easier and an even easier version)	Activity	30 min	43
Recording colour mixing	Skill	45 min	45
Mixing and recording colours: browns	Skill	45 min	46
Mixing and painting in browns	Using Skill	45 min	48
Mixing and painting in different whites	Using Skill	1 hour	49
Adding black to make a darker colour tone	Skill	2 hours	50
Creating skin tones	Skill	30 min	51
Painting a self-portrait using skin tones	Using Skill	1 hour	52
Using a range of colours in a painting	Using Skill	45 min	53
Colour matching	Skill	1 hour	54
Colour theory			
Background information			56
Key aspects of colour theory			58
The colour wheel	Key Skill	45 min to 1 hour	59
Revisiting and extending knowledge of colour theory	Key Skill	1 hour	60
Painting using colour theory	Using Skill	1 hour	61
Trying out different colour combinations	Using Skill	1 hour	62
Assessing knowledge of colour and colour theory			63

A skills-based approach to painting

For children as young artists, painting can be a means of personal expression, a way to express ideas and feelings.

All artists experiment with colour and use materials in a personal way. This book aims to enable teachers to support children in this same process of discovery and exploration.

The use of paint needs to be taught to children; they need to be led to an awareness of colour and how it can be mixed and used in order for them to grow in confidence and in understanding in the handling of paint. They should know it can be applied in layers or changed, and that its surface can be flat or textured. They should know that different qualities of paint may be used for different purposes.

Younger pupils will generally paint without inhibition, but as children progress through the school they will need direct teaching in order for them to master the media and to develop skills. The originality, the individual vision and inspiration will come from them. However formally they are taught, their creativity will not be impaired and they will still evolve their own style and have their own ideas.

How the skills-based approach works

Painting is essentially about colour and paints and the way in which these are controlled and used. In this book, these aspects are taken apart and pared down to their basic elements. They have been separated initially into simple lessons which show children how particular types of paint behave and the different ways in which colours can be mixed and used.

The skills acquired should be used in a context as soon as possible, not only for purposes of consolidation, but also so that children will be able to see how these skills can be used in a painting and how they will increase the effectiveness of their work.

Marie Roberts, Year 4

The skills and experiences should build over time to help children develop the confidence and competence they need to create the effects they desire. They should to be able to express their own ideas and feelings effectively in paint and colour. Confidence in the process and in themselves is essential if they are going to gain the benefits of being able to take pleasure in it and communicate through this medium.

One way to achieve this confidence is to help children achieve control over the paints and the tools. They should also be encouraged to see opportunities to change and develop their work when they use these skills in the context of a painting.

Children need to realize that adult artists also had to learn and practise basic techniques and that they themselves are now involved in the same process.

Learning to paint is as difficult as learning any other complex discipline. One way we can help children not to be overwhelmed with the task is to limit the choices of media and colours and to be specific about the focus of the painting session.

Paints have different properties and children should be given experience of a wide range, although they should not be introduced to too many at once because this will confuse them. It is to be recommended that the school has one staple paint medium that will be used consistently throughout the school, with other painting media being used alongside this as appropriate.

Children's skills will develop more successfully if the teacher introduces painting tools and media systematically, and encourages children to experiment, whilst providing learning tasks that are challenging. In this way, it is possible to build their skills and confidence step by step until they are equipped to launch out on their own with less and less teacher intervention.

In this book, the staple paint is powder paint, with ready-mixed paint figuring mainly with the younger age groups. However, a wide range of other painting media are introduced at various stages throughout the book.

Looking at the work of other artists to see how they have dealt with colour and paint is an integral part of this approach to the teaching of painting. It helps children to recognize that they are young artists struggling with the same essential elements of painting – colour, shape, tone, texture and movement – as all adult artists, past and present.

When looking at works of art, children can be told, 'This is what artists do. They look at each other's work for inspiration and solutions, and they take ideas and change them. This is what they have always done; it is why artists often like to work and live near other artists. A creative person can take an idea and turn it into something which is his or her own.'

Few children in a school will become professional artists, but an appreciation of art and of colour is life-enhancing.

Jack Muirhead, Year 3

Progression

In an ideal world, there would be consistency and continuity in the approach to painting throughout the school. The order of the content of the art curriculum will vary according to the school's own planning, but the principle behind the teaching in this book is that the skill/medium/technique is introduced and taught and is then used in a painting context as soon as possible. This could be the same day, the next art session, or whenever is appropriate to the skill.

Children will need regular opportunities to experiment with a new medium so that they have a chance to examine its potential. Successful use of a new skill or medium boosts a child's self-esteem and builds confidence to experiment.

Whereas there are some media that are more age-appropriate than others (for example, oil painting is generally better saved for older Key Stage 2 children), it is as well, where possible, to give all ages the opportunity to experiment with different media and materials. Older junior children can make stunning mono prints from finger paintings, whilst young infants respond well to the challenge of painting with tiny brushes.

Dominic Cork, Year 3

Painting should be tackled in terms of what is possible and appropriate to the medium. Learning about paint is a gradual process, beginning in school at foundation stage and developing in complexity as understanding grows.

This should be enhanced from the earliest years by the introduction of works of art. Children should be invited to respond and to develop a vocabulary of response. The questioning from the teacher should become more probing and specific as the years go by, starting with simple questioning about what the children can see and what they like or don't like about a work of art, and progressing to such thoughts as 'what the artist's intention might have been'.

Examples of a range of questioning in response to works of art is to be found on page 99 in the chapter on Using works of art.

Children's development in painting

Children first use colour at an intuitive and emotional or convenience level, because they like it, because it looks right or because it was handy and there was some left.

Children tend to express what they know rather than what they see, which is why skies tend to be blue at the top of the page and grass green at the bottom, with an area of white left in between. The appearance of a yellow quarter section of a sun in the top right- or left-hand corner is really just a symbol which the child knows will be recognized and 'read' by whoever views the painting. They become quite surprised if they are questioned about why they put it there and when they last saw a sun like this.

This schematic approach to painting a scene should really not appear later than Year 3, unless the child is very immature, as then it is really just a form of laziness. As they mature, they become more aware of the complexity of the visual environment and the problems of interpreting the 'real' world.

When children become aware of the difference between the images they paint and those they see around them, they can lose satisfaction with what they have produced and it becomes important to them that their images are acceptable to others as well as themselves.

As young children develop an awareness of space, the random earlier daubs are replaced by a more considered representation. At this stage there is no concept of scale and the child exaggerates and distorts to emphasize things of personal significance and importance. As co-ordination increases, children extend their range of symbols and execute paintings with more detail, together with a diminishing size of their work.

Experience and progression of skills over 2 years

Year 3

* Learns about colour theory and how artists use it
* Explores links between colour and feelings
* Knows the order of colours in the spectrum
* Learns to choose brushes appropriate to the task
* Experiments with mark making, using cotton buds, twigs, feathers, etc as well as brushes
* Uses other media in paintings, eg collage
* Paints objects and models: papier-mâché, clay items, etc
* Paints on wood, stone and a variety of surfaces
* Studies the history of painting and tries some styles and techniques
* Extends vocabulary of response to works of art
* Mixes powder paint and uses one pure colour in a full range of tones from deepest to the palest tone using only water (no white paint)
* Does the same activity with watercolours
* Learns a little of the history of colours and paint
* Explores watercolours and learns the names and properties of the paint
* Colour mixes in watercolours and explores unusual combinations (yellow and black to create olive green, purple and yellow to create brown, etc) for realism
* Learns about movements in art, eg impressionism
* Extends vocabulary in relation to works of art, eg background, foreground, horizon
* Extends vocabulary of response to works of art and formulates own questioning using appropriate terms
* Is introduced to the concept of composition and looks at it in terms of works of art
* Plans own painting, thinking about where to start and where things might go
* Considers background as part of a whole composition
* Colour matches to objects and other images

By the end of Year 4

* Revises colour theory and extends vocabulary to include complementary, harmonious and earth colours
* Paints in monochrome
* Studies works of art that are executed in a restricted palette, eg Picasso's blue period or scenes by LS Lowry
* Studies works of art from other cultures and people in history in terms of colours, styles and materials
* Extends the period of time over which a piece of work is sustained
* Lays a wash in watercolour and lifts off colour using cotton wool
* Works on both wet and damp paper
* Experiments in colour mixing in powder and watercolour and records results
* Investigates acrylic paints
* Uses metallic paint to paint 3-D objects
* Paints in the style of another artist, using their brush strokes, techniques or colours
* Paints in the style of an art movement, eg Pointillism
* Revision of mark making always relevant

Dominic Cork, Year 3

Resources

In an ideal world, a well-stocked art cupboard might contain:

Different types of paint
* Ready-mixed
* Powder paint
* Tempera paint (blocks and tablets)
* Watercolours (blocks in tins)
* Watercolours: powdered (Brusho®)
* Poster paint
* Metallic
* Pearlescent
* Cromar
* Fabric paint
* Acrylic
* Gouache
* Marbling
* Emulsion (for large-scale work)

Drawing media
* Watercolour pencils
* Water-soluble crayons
* Charcoal
* Oil pastel
* Art (chalky) pastels
* Felt tips
* Permanent ink pens

Brushes
* Long- and short-handled stiff-bristled brushes in different sizes and tips
* Watercolour brushes in various sizes
* Decorator brushes in various sizes

Papers
As well as the usual paper that a primary school keeps:
* Cartridge paper, ready-cut in various sizes
* Kitchen paper
* Junior art paper
* Thin card (for acrylics)
* Blotting paper

Sundry items
* Brush holders
* Paint wells (for powder paint)
* Sketchbooks
* Palettes (various types to suit the paint being used)
* Water pots
* Protective clothing
* Painting storage racks (for drying)
* Masking tape

Technical painting terms

The painter's materials are called 'media' and include, for example, oils, watercolours, acrylics, etc.

These media are applied to a 'support', such as canvas, wood, paper, using a variety of tools such as brushes, palette knife and fingers. Below the surface of a painting there may be other layers of paint, usually called an 'under-painting', and beneath the painting there may also be an 'under-drawing'.

Explanation of other painting terms can be found in the glossary on pages 113–115.

More detailed information about each resource such as colours, sizes, quantities, types available, etc and advice starts on the following page.

Specific information about each type of paint comes in its own chapter or in a particular lesson.

Hayley Henry, Year 5 (the Mona Lisa)

Paints

Finger paints
These usually come ready-mixed in re-sealable pots; they are available in bright colours, in black and white and with glitter.

Ready-mixed
This is useful for younger children, as powder paint is more difficult to mix, but it is also very useful for larger-scale work for all ages and for painting models.

It has its limitations for colour mixing, and children tend to dip into colours and use them as they are. As with most paints, it is advisable to order double the quantity of white and yellow.

Metallic paint
It is better to buy this in ready-mixed form as the powdered variety can be difficult to mix up. There are two grades of ready-mixed paint: Meltdown paint, which is more expensive but is suited to smaller-scale work and is excellent for painting small clay models; and less expensive varieties which are not so glorious when dry but which are quite suitable for general use and for younger children.

Pearlescent
These water-based paints have a lovely shimmer and add a different dimension to a painting. They are also useful for painting models, and particularly for clay models if the school does not have a kiln to fire glazes.

Cromar
These are translucent water-based paints that can be used on any surface but are ideal for use on glass or plastic.

Tempera (block) paint
Tempera comes in solid blocks and needs to be thoroughly moistened before use. The blocks – flat cylindrical tablets that fit into a palette – need to be of a good quality, otherwise it is difficult to make paint of a covering consistency. They have limited use when colours need to be mixed as they generally end up with other colours over the top and have to be cleaned before they can be used next time. No lessons in this medium are included in this book.

Tempera paints are quick to set out and are not messy to clear up, so they can be useful when the classroom has no sink, and younger children do not find them daunting. However, they are not sufficient to be the only paint available.

Powder paint
Powder paint is the best painting medium in the primary school. It allows full and sensitive colour mixing and is reasonably priced. It comes in dry form and children can mix it themselves, but the process needs to be taught. The best aspect of powder paint is that it is possible to mix an almost limitless range of colours. It is not necessary to stock more than six colours plus black and white.

The downside of using powder paint is that it can be difficult for children to mix a large amount of a blended colour, and they need to develop their skills in using it. They will also need direct teaching and support to get the right consistency. There is more about this in the chapter on basic skills (pages 25–26 and 29).

Watercolour
This comes in three forms: tablet, tube and powder. The tablets can be bought separately or ready placed in tins which have a lid that can be used for colour mixing. The tubes are more expensive and are really only suitable for older Key Stage 2 children who have had experience of working with tablets.

The powder is very versatile and is excellent for large washes, wax resist and for use on fabrics, especially batik. The most common brand is Brusho®. It is not colour-fast and will wash out. It can be mixed with water to any density of colour and can be stored in screw-top jars for later use. It can also be sprinkled directly onto damp paper for an unusual effect. It comes in small tubs and will stain the skin under your fingernails, so it is advisable to wear latex gloves when mixing it.

Watercolours become translucent when applied thinly.

Peter Rodgers, Year 4

Poster paint

This water-based paint comes in small pots or tubes and does not really do anything that good quality ready-mixed paint does not.

Fabric paint

There are a variety of fabric paints available from different suppliers. There are colour-fast varieties and also some that come in crayon form. Some need ironing to make them colour-fast. They come in all colours, including fluorescent and pearlescent types.

Acrylic paint

Acrylic paint is a thick, creamy paint sold in large tubes or pots. Acrylics can be diluted with water but have a plastic base which forms a waterproof skin. The paint peels off skin but does not come out of clothes, and for this reason it is not really suitable for Key Stage 1 use unless the children are closely supervised.

Acrylic paint can be built up in layers, can be over-painted once dry without mixing colours, and can be used to create texture. It can be applied with a brush or a palette knife.

Particular care has to be taken when using acrylic paint as it is also a strong adhesive. Paintbrushes need to be cleaned immediately after the painting session has finished or they will set rock hard and have to be thrown away.

Gouache

Gouache is an opaque watercolour; the pigment is thickened with white chalk. It is not really necessary in primary school unless a particular project requires it, although it is a useful medium for graphic design. It comes in tubes.

Ink

Ink is a transparent dye. Inks come in beautiful colours for ink and wash work. You really only need black, although sepia is lovely to use. A little goes a long way. Brusho® (powdered watercolour) can be used in place of ink if it is mixed with only a small amount of water. Check the label on the ink bottle to make sure it is safe for children to use.

Marbling inks

Marbling inks are special oil-based colours. They float on the surface of water, and paper can be laid on top to pick up the patterns of the swirling colours. They are relatively foolproof and children love the effects created. However, the children need to wear protective clothing.

Emulsion paint

Household emulsion paint is good for large-scale work, internal murals or scenery. It is less expensive than ready-mixed paint and some types are wipeable.

Care needs to be taken that the instructions on the tin state that it is safe for children to use. Many children have very sensitive skins.

Thomas Stodgel, Year 3 (a red bird)

Drawing media

Watercolour pencils
These are artists' quality coloured pencils. Lovely colour blending effects can be achieved with them and the children's drawings can be wet with a brush so the colours move and blend. They are particularly useful in plant studies.

Water-soluble crayons
These are used in the same way as watercolour pencils.

Felt tips
Most felt-tip pens can be used as described for watercolour pencils. They are also interesting to use to show colour separation when spots of colour are drawn onto wet blotting paper and left for the colours to spread and separate.

Permanent ink pens
These generally come in three thicknesses and the thicker points can be round- or chisel-ended.

These are excellent for drawing over paintings (examples of this can be found on pages 16 and 20). They work well over watercolours, but care needs to be taken when using them over thick powder paint or ready-mixed paint, because the pen points can clog, and they do not work well over wet paint. Permanent pens are also good for drawing beneath paintings as the ink does not run.

Charcoal
Charcoal drawings can be wet with a brush and the black will move to make shades of grey. This is a classic medium and has a long history.

Artists' pastels
Chalky pastels can be used in the same way as charcoal. Using sepia or burnt sienna pastels can give an 'old look' to a painting. This might be appropriate when studying artists such as Leonardo da Vinci, for example.

Brushes
It is important to offer the children a range of brushes, both small and large. House painting brushes are also useful for covering large areas and for certain techniques such as spatter painting. Brushes need to be looked after, washed out after use and never stored brush-end downward in a container. This is particularly important with short-handled watercolour brushes as these are virtually unusable once the ends have become bent. Store brushes which are to be used for acrylics and oils separately.

Children need to be taught good brush techniques, ie how to hold them just above the ferrule (metal band) with a similar hold to pencils, and not to scrub with them, which splays the hairs. This shortens their life (the brushes not the children, although if I catch them at it…!!).

Children should also be encouraged not to leave their brushes standing in water pots, but to rinse them and lay them across their palettes or on the table, even when the lesson is paused for further information and teaching. It is prudent to make this the normal practice so it becomes second nature. Brushes' points, particularly watercolour brush points, become misshapen when left standing in water.

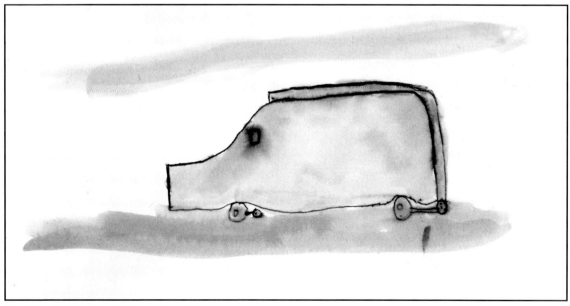

Charlotte Hastie, Year 3 (line and wash)

Different brush strokes can be made with different ends. A range of good brushes in different sizes is essential if pupils are to be able to master the process of painting. Different media require different brushes.

General-use brushes: ready-mixed paint, powder and acrylics

Hog hair is the cheapest option and adequate for most uses; the downside is that they tend to be softer and can lose their hair. Synthetic hair is also available. This is more expensive, but it keeps its shape well and is more economical in the long run.

Brushes are generally long-handled and are available in a range of thicknesses from size 4 to size 18.

For general use, the round ends are adequate, but it is good to have a few sizes of flat-ended brushes as well for painting with textured paint. A brush with a square end will produce a different effect from a round one. In order to gain confidence in the use of a range of brushes, it is good to encourage pupils to experiment with their differing effects, recording the outcomes in their sketchbooks.

Watercolour brushes

The best brushes, like the best paints, tend to be the most expensive. The cheaper brushes are really not worth bothering with; they will just make it more difficult for children to achieve control over this tricky medium.

Year 4 pupil

If the art budget will run to sable, get that type and then make sure the children value them and look after them. If not, then buy the best you can afford.

A range of sizes is again important, the smallest is size 0 and the range goes up to size 12. The larger ones are good for washes and the small to medium ones for detail.

Watercolour brushes need to be looked after and should be kept separately and stored with care – never brush-end downward in a pot.

Brush storage

There are ready-made brush stands available from different suppliers. It can be a bit fiddly to put the brushes in some of them, but this can always be done by an art monitor. Otherwise, cleaned brushes can be stored flat in trays or wooded ends down in pots in their different sizes.

Children should be encouraged to choose the most appropriate brush for the job in hand, particularly in terms of size. Frequently, children will try to cover large areas with a tiny brush or try to paint in minute detail with a large brush. If a range of brush sizes is available to them on their table from the onset of the session, they will be more likely to independently choose the best one for their purpose.

Other methods of paint application

It is important to point out that brushes are not the only method of applying paint to a surface. Most children enjoy inventing and making their own painting implements. There is an example of this on page 88 in the chapter on History of painting.

Children should, where possible, be given the opportunity to experiment with such things as fingers, sponges, rags, cotton buds, strips of card and rollers.

Twigs and feathers, rags and cotton wool can be used to lift off paint as well as apply it.

Texture

Fabric can be pressed into wet paint to create a texture in a painting. Thick paint can be applied with a plastic or palette knife to create a rough, uneven texture which is called 'impasto'.

Various substances can be added to paint to make it thicker or textured, such as PVA, sawdust, salt, starch, flour, icing sugar, crushed egg shells, sand or Polyfilla®.

Paint applied thickly can be scraped with twigs or the ends of brushes to make lines and marks in the paint.

Bits and pieces can be dropped onto thick, wet paint, such as dry grass, sand, sawdust, tissue paper, foil, thin fabric, netting or glitter.

Paper

Shape
Artists have terms for which way round paper is to be used. 'Portrait' refers to having the long side vertical, while 'landscape' refers to the longer side being horizontal.

Quality
Good quality paper is essential if the paint is to adhere satisfactorily to the surface and if the paper is to remain flat after drying. If the paper is too thin, it may well not absorb moisture and may cockle when dry, spoiling the look of the work. Newsprint, cheap sugar paper and shiny paper are unsatisfactory and should be avoided except, perhaps, as test paper for colour mixing.

Paper is sold not only in sizes but also by weight. The weight of one square metre of paper in grams is written as GSM or g/sm: the larger the number, the stronger and firmer the paper. 70–170 g/sm is the range most school suppliers carry.

It is useful to order the paper you need in manageable sizes, unless you need the largest size for large-scale or group work. The very large sheets are difficult to store and often become damaged when other paper is removed or replaced. Separate packs of A1, A2, A3 and A4, ready-cut in the weight you need, are useful. Larger pieces have to be cut to size and there is not always enough time to fiddle about. As art is such a resource-heavy subject, collecting and setting out a range of media before a lesson can be daunting. Locating the guillotine, finding a space to put it on and cutting up the paper take time.

Sketchbooks should be of the best quality paper that the art budget can run to; not only is it better for drawing on but it will hold the paint and mean children can work directly into their books when necessary.

Types of paper
Kitchen paper
Thin, cheap paper, also known as 'fish and chip' paper, is not an ideal surface for paint. It goes soggy quickly, it cockles, and the colours disappear into it. It is acceptable for early

years work because these children do so many paintings, sometimes consisting of just a few brush strokes. In this case it would be expensive to use good quality cartridge paper all the time.

Cartridge
Cartridge paper is so called because it was made strong and firm in order to make cartridges for gunpowder. 115 g/sm is a good medium weight for general use, while 135 g/sm is better for acrylics and watercolours.

Junior art paper
Junior art paper is a light-weight paper and is quite useful for general use.

Watercolour papers
Watercolour paper is expensive. It is rougher and stiffer than other papers, but it holds the paint well and won't bubble up when it is wetted. Children could practise skills on good quality cartridge and, when it comes to their final paintings, watercolour paper could be used.

Pre-prepared backgrounds
Backgrounds should not always be white, nor always plain. It is good to give the children the opportunity to paint on coloured, patterned and textured surfaces.

Harriet Gregory, Year 3

Backgrounds can be:
* Wet, damp or dry
* Screwed up and smoothed out
* Rollered, using printing or decorator's rollers, with paint or printing ink
* Collaged
* Painted
* Printed in different ways, eg screwed-up cling film, bubble wrap or fabric
* Colour-washed using thin paints or inks
* Textured, such as wallpaper, sandpaper or woodchip.

Canvas and canvas board

Most oil paintings are painted on canvas, but children can use acrylics on them, too. A canvas is usually a piece of linen cloth that has been stretched over a frame or board and then protected with a primer. Canvas board is cheaper, but small canvases can be purchased quite inexpensively at many high street outlets nowadays, and this may prove better value than art or school suppliers.

Other surfaces and finishes

Paint can be applied to many different surfaces, such as cardboard, chipboard, wood, stone, etc. Some surfaces, however, need specialist paint – ceramics and glass, for example, and also fabric if it is to be washed and the colours not fade.

Year 4 pupil

Children could paint on walls, doors, benches, trees, on fabric or on plastic. Old shoes, containers and furniture can be transformed.

Clear PVA can be over-painted to make artwork waterproof (up to a point), or varnishes can be applied to make colours brighter. I have heard that furniture polish can be sprayed over powder paint paintings and then buffed to bring out the colours.

Other resources

Water pots

Water pots need to be stable and stackable. The type with a wider base than top are the best, and also don't need a lid. The pots must be tall enough to hold long-handled brushes so that they don't fall out. You will need enough for one between two children and plenty of spares for other purposes, such as holding quantities of ready-mixed paint or mixed-up Brusho® (powdered watercolour).

Palettes

There are several different varieties of palettes available from suppliers, but many teachers just use old plates. It depends really upon what suits your purpose and what you personally prefer to use.

Palettes need to be easy to wash out quickly, so curved edges to the hollows are helpful. They also need to stack and not take up too much room on the table. Unless you are lucky enough to have an art room with lots of table space for each child, you will need to consider carefully the space on the table for paints, palettes, water pots and whatever other resources are being used.

Plastic moulded palettes with nine wells are excellent for colour mixing, as they give enough space for a range of colours and are big enough to share between two. Palettes are also available with six wells.

The disadvantage of mixing paint on single flat surfaces, like plates or trays, is that it is difficult to keep the colours separated and they tend to run together.

Watercolours can be mixed in the lids of the paint boxes, on an old plate, on palettes with smaller wells; a stiff piece of shiny card will do if you are really stuck.

It is possible to buy special paper palettes for acrylics, and this may save a lot of time on clearing up.

A tip which saves water and washing-up time is to put a piece of cling film over the palette. At the end of the painting session, pull off the cling film and throw it away. This leaves the palettes clean and does not pour chemicals into the water system.

Easels

It is good for children to have the experience of working at an easel at some stage in their school life. This generally happens at lower Key Stage 1 when children have a selection of ready-mixed colours in pots along the bottom of an easel tray. While it is good to be able to stand back from your work and view it at a distance, the disadvantage is that, unless it is very thick, the paint tends to run down the paper. Once the children have dipped their brushes in the water to clean them, the paint becomes thin and watery and will dribble down the page.

If you have a large art room, you might invest in a few collapsible easels which store easily. A group of older children could then try the experience of working, standing half an arm's length from the easel, and they could also try holding the paintbrush further along the handle than usual. This would really only be for suitable for oil, acrylic or thickened paints.

Drying racks

There are several different types available, pretty much all of them fiddly and tricky in different ways. The ones with loose, moveable shelves are particularly maddening as the shelves tend to come away in your hand when you are holding a wet painting in the other. Others have shelves which, after a few years of use, tend to slope downwards (children have been known to lean on them and speed this tendency), so inevitably the wet paintings all slide off the shelves. Fun!

Drying racks take up quite a bit of space in a classroom unless wall-mounted, and they can become dumping grounds; however, they are essential in order to have somewhere to put wet artwork and to stop it becoming dog-eared and damaged. If the racks are accessible to children, they can carry their own work to the rack, but this can be fraught with danger. Wet artwork often runs unless children remember to carry it horizontally, and there is always the danger of them bumping into a child who isn't wearing a painting overall, thereby smearing them with paint. This is naturally always a child who has a very particular parent!

Some drying racks have lift-up shelves, while others have pull-out shelves, and some are on wheels so they can be removed from the classroom.

Pegging artwork up on washing lines or clothes drying racks is a popular solution and can work well unless paint is wet and running.

Protective clothing

This is another area fraught with difficulty, so here are a few suggestions.

An old adult-sized T-shirt makes an excellent painting overall. It has no buttons or strings and slips on easily. It covers most of the arms and the body, and comes down to the thighs or even lower. You could purchase 30 or so new T-shirts quite cheaply, probably at no more than a pound each, whereas you could spend the whole year asking children to bring them in from home and get only a few responses.

The school could buy painting overalls or aprons for each class, but it is only worthwhile getting the better quality ones, which can work out expensive. You would also need to get several different sizes. Cheaper aprons, however, are a waste of time as they rip or split very quickly.

Whichever way you do it, the children need to protect their clothes for most painting lessons.

Jessica Hewit, Year 4

Classroom organization

The first consideration in classroom organization is, 'how many children are going to be painting at one time?' This determines how much equipment is needed. Sometimes children may paint in smaller groups, with the activity rotating over the day or week, until everyone that should have had a go at the activity has had their turn. However, it is quite likely that, for various reasons, there will be times when the whole class is painting at the same time.

The greater the number of children painting at the same time, the more crucial it is that the equipment is organized efficiently. Children can then achieve optimum benefit from the experience and will not have to battle against the mess and muddle that can ensue quickly when equipment is not organized with care and consideration.

Many teachers shudder at the thought of a whole class of young children all painting at the same time, but it is manageable and it does have some advantages. It provides a whole-class experience, and the shared sense of discovery and achievement can be powerful. It does 'get it over with' in one go, and with such a crowded

curriculum there is no longer time for things to drag out over several weeks. Also, with smaller groups each taking their own turn to paint, the moment can pass and the activity may lose its impact, or a topical aspect may no longer apply. There are also display implications: do you wait until all the children have done it before the artwork goes up on the wall? The younger the children, the sooner they want to see their work displayed or to take it home.

The following are a few pointers that apply whatever the size of the group, and regardless of where the art materials are kept – whether they are in your classroom, stored in some central location or, if your school is big enough, in an art room.

Newspaper
If you cover tables with newspaper, two layers is best. The advantage of this is that it absorbs some spills, extra layers can be added if necessary and damp brushes can be dried on it. Newspaper can be cleared quickly away at the end of the session and, unless there have been a lot of spills, tables should not even need wiping. If the children are setting out newspaper themselves, then check that it does not poke out beyond the edges of the table. This can cause disasters in that, when anyone walks past the table, they are in danger of catching it against themselves and inadvertently swiping the whole contents of the table onto the floor.

One last point about newspapers: broadsheets do the job best. It takes less time to lay them out as the pages are bigger and there are fewer 'unsuitable' images. Even so, keep an eye out for disturbing images that might distress children – for example, from war zones or of natural disasters. Just flip those pages over.

Setting out tables
Consider paper size before setting out the tables; if children are working with A2 or A3 paper, then fewer of them can work at a time. If it is group work on a large-scale surface, you may have to leave space around the edge of the table for materials, or place them on a table nearby. Where there are implications for different media, these will be covered in the relevant lesson. Otherwise, for a table of children working on individual work, set out:

Year 3 pupil

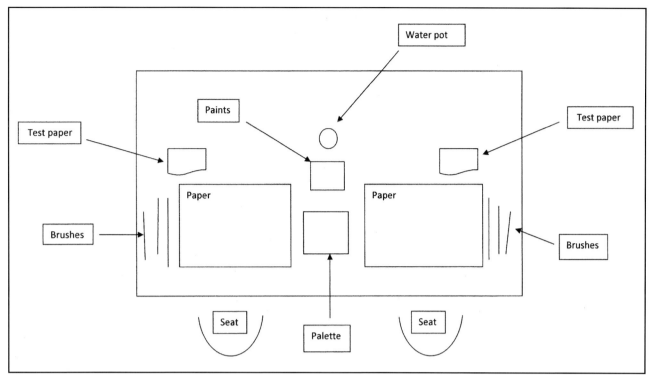

A table set out for two children

❋ Paper for artwork
❋ Enough water pots and paints and palettes positioned so that children do not have to reach across each other to get to them (this causes water and paint to land on their paintings when it shouldn't)
❋ A test paper for each child to try out colours and dab brushes on
❋ A pencil, for writing the child's name on the back of their work, if nothing else
❋ At least one brush per child, or possibly a selection of brushes of different sizes.

As a general rule, one water pot and one palette between two children works well. This may vary according to the activity and the size of the palettes.

Consider what other resources need to be on the table, eg items to be depicted, other art media or sketchbooks and where they can be best placed. Sketchbooks take up a lot of room; if children are using these for reference, they could put them under their chairs while they are not looking at them.

Remember that children will also need protective clothing (see page 17).

There is more specific information about setting out different media in chapters relating to that particular medium.

Changing dirty paint water
As children work more independently, they can be encouraged to change their own water when they think it needs changing. It can be explained to them that although their water may look dirty, it only needs changing if, when they put a clean brush in the water and then dab it onto their test paper, it shows up as a colour rather than just a wet mark. If it shows up as a colour, then tell them to change it

Consideration for others
Children should be encouraged to help set out, clear away and clean up, in whatever way is appropriate to their age, and they should also be taught to keep their work space clean. If this becomes messy, not only is their own artwork in danger of getting ruined but so is other children's work. They will need to be taught to look after the brushes and to consider the needs of other children who are sharing the materials.

Clearing up
Oh dear, the dreaded clearing-up time! This is not so bad if you have adult help, but for a number of reasons this may not be available. If you do not have a teaching assistant, or you do have one but they are not free to assist, a willing parent helper is a boon. Failing all these options, however, you will just have to pack up a bit earlier and have a simple activity organized to keep the children busy whilst you deal with the clearing up. It could be you at the sink or an adult helper.

Here are a few suggestions and a sequence of clearing-up activities:

* Have no more than four 'monitors'.
* Say, 'No one is to get up from their seats unless I have asked them to', otherwise the room will be full of children milling about with water pots, etc, getting in each other's way or getting into mischief.
* Clear up one group at a time and leave the others still working.
* Remove artwork first and put it somewhere safe. Clearing-up time is the most likely time for something disastrous to happen to it.
* Remove paints.
* Don't let children carry powder paint around, because sooner or later they will drop it or will trip up and send it flying. It will go everywhere.
* Collect brushes and drop them into the sink (even if children have washed them, they will still generally need another wash). Leave them there while the water pots are rinsed.
* Collect the water pots next and wash them up, stacking them upside-down to drain. These take up the most room in the sink and so are best got rid of first.

* Wash the brushes and stand them to drain in a water pot or two.
* Collect palettes and dump them in the sink to soak (NB see note about palettes and cling film on page 17).
* While the palettes are soaking, remove any other paint from the tables.
* Collect test papers.
* Remove newspaper.
* Send that group to wash their hands and put away their aprons, and give them their next activity.
* Wash the palettes, which, by now, will not be so difficult to clean. Children will need to be taught how to clean palettes. Getting the tap turned on at the right pressure is key to this, as is holding the palettes under running water at an angle away from themselves.
* Repeat the clearing-up routine with the next group.

This is not as bad as it sounds. If, whenever possible, the children have something to do, it should run fairly smoothly. There will be times when they will have to just sit there patiently for a few moments with nothing to do during clearing up, but that can't be helped.

If you have no sink (poor you!). Try using three buckets:

* One with clean water to fill water pots
* One empty for dirty brushes and paint water
* One half full of water to soak palettes; better still use some kind of disposable palettes.

Keeping artwork

Younger children usually want to take their work home as soon as possible, but you may want to display some of it, and you might also want to keep a few examples for school records or for your own future reference. These can be stored in large polythene window display books or in a home-made sugar paper display book.

You, or the art co-ordinator, might want evidence of coverage and progression for a number of reasons. A sample of artwork with a few notes attached about resources, planning, focus, etc can be valuable for future use. A glance at the artwork alone can be enough to remind you what you did and enable you to do it again at a later date.

If you want to be really organized, you could also keep labels from the display with the artwork and file it somewhere others could access it.

Laura Dennis, Year 3

Starting points and ideas for themes, topics or inspiration

Before you start painting

Backgrounds

Before you start any artwork, some consideration should be given to the background. Children should not always work on white, or even plain, paper.

The surface they work on, be it paper, card or whatever, could be coloured, patterned or textured. This might be ready-made or prepared by the children themselves.

Backgrounds can be printed, children could roll inked rollers over them in different colours, they might have been ragged (printed with screwed-up rags dipped in paint), textured, or they might be wet or dampened. Paper could be screwed up and then smoothed out again before it is worked on, or even screwed up, ironed after a first layer of paint is applied and then painted again.

It is important for children to consider backgrounds as part of their paintings, not just the white bits behind their picture.

Year 3 children might be encouraged to 'fill in the background with a colour', but older children should really start considering their backgrounds from the onset. They need to think about what might be in them and what colours they might be, as part of their whole composition.

Discussion and observation

Painting from observation – from looking at and representing what exists, as opposed to painting abstract feelings and moods – is easier if children have the opportunity to study how something looks. Whether this is through the work or from first-hand experience depends on the subject matter.

Painting from imagination is quite difficult for older children, because they are usually striving for realism and realism is difficult if there is no opportunity to examine how something actually looks. If it is not possible for whatever reason to look at the real thing, then the Internet is an excellent resource. If you have an interactive whiteboard, open up the Google search engine and click on 'Images'. If you then type in

whatever it is you want to look at, eg dragons, it will bring up an enormous selection of images for you to select and enlarge on the screen. There is usually a 'see full size image' option to click on, which will make the image larger so that all the children can see it.

Children can be directed to look at the basic shape of the subject, the colour, the surface texture, where the light falls, the darkest and lightest areas, etc.

They should also be encouraged to look at their environment and be given opportunities to express their ideas, thoughts and feelings about it.

The more children observe, handle and discuss the things they are going to paint, the more detailed their work will be. Before starting painting, encourage discussion and questions about the nature of the task, the objectives and the skills involved.

Oliver Squire, Year 3

21

Points for children to consider

When we ask children to make paintings, we may underestimate how many decisions have to be made and how many choices there are to be made.

When making a painting, here are just some of the points children might have to consider:

* What will the content of the painting be?
* Will the painting have a particular mood or feeling?
* What resources are needed to support the content of the painting?
* What type of background is needed?
* Will the background be one colour or several?
* Is the background an important part of the composition or is it neutral?
* What surface is the painting to be on?
* Will the surface be wet/damp or dry?
* Thinking and planning the composition of the painting.
* Whether to make some kind of preliminary drawing or marks.
* Where is a good place to begin the painting?
* What brush(es) will be needed for different parts of the painting?
* Which colour to start with?
* How much paint needs to be mixed to get started?
* Is the paint mixed to the desired consistency?
* Does one area need to be dry before it is worked on, or worked next to?
* What will happen to the under-layer of paint, if it is painted over?
* How will special effects be created?
* How will the impression of fur/foliage/distance/warmth, etc be created?
* Is it better to put in small details later?
* Can a desired effect be achieved by using special brush marks?
* Will texture be used, in part or all over?
* How does the painting look from a distance?
* Does it 'read' (make sense to the viewer)?
* Does anything need changing to improve the painting?
* Does the painting need to be finished in one session?
* Is the painting finished?

Jordan Wild, Year 4 (landscape with fields)

Experiences and stimuli for paintings

* Responding to excursions and outings
* Interpreting music, poetry, stories and drama
* Studying nature and man-made objects in the everyday world
* Investigating art materials
* Interpreting personal experiences, feelings and moods.

Starting-points and subject ideas

* Animals, fish, insects
* Plants: flowers, trees, grasses, etc
* Interiors, views through windows/doors, family scenes
* Domestic objects, food and utensils, furniture, still life
* Buildings past and present, doors, roofs, windows, bricks
* Landscapes, rural and urban
* Water: sea, lakes, rivers
* Natural disasters: volcanoes, tidal waves, etc
* Portraits: self, individual, groups, miniatures
* Fantasy: dragons, fairies, magic, mystery, wizards, etc
* Dreams, wishes, nightmares
* The future: transport, clothes, homes
* Space: travel, planets, sun, moon, etc
* Toys, games, past and present
* Fire: candles, flames, etc
* Light, shade, shadows, contrast
* Reflection: in water, in glass, on curved surfaces
* Weather: storm, rain, sun, wind, heat, cold, snow, frost
* Seasons: characteristics and colours
* Camouflage in animals, insects, birds, fish, etc
* Multicultural life and culture
* Artefacts linked to topics, history, science, etc
* Transport: cars, lorries, motorbikes, wheels, aeroplanes, trains
* Roads, road markings, traffic, street lights
* Underground: caves, creatures, tunnels
* Myths and legends
* Entertainment: circus, theatre, dance, music, puppets, fairs
* Sports and games: clothing, equipment, stars, Olympics

* Machines: cogs, chains, tools, engines, fantasy
* Advertising: magazines, television, hoardings, packaging
* Growth: animal, human, plant, communities
* Industry: factories, workers, canals, chimneys
* Clothing: fashion, costumes, fabrics, hats, shoes, past and present
* Past cultures: Egypt, Greece, etc
* Celebrations: birthdays, weddings, parties
* Food, drink
* Patterns: natural and man-made
* Movement: animal, human, speed, clouds, wind
* Habitats: jungle, desert, under stones, Arctic, etc
* Families: animal, human, plants, objects
* Time: clocks, watches, ageing
* Decorative arts: ceramics, weaving, jewellery.

Jay Latham, Year 4

Basic skills

Roger Aggyman, Year 4

24

Introducing powder paint

Why powder paint?

Powder colour is by far the best choice for colour mixing because it gives children the best opportunity to control the process of mixing and changing colour. Dry colour cannot be used straight from the pot; water has to be added and this involves children with the process from the onset.

Success depends on children having been taught powder paint handling as a specific skill. If it is taught in a separate session when the focus is dealing with the medium rather than creating a painting, then children are only fighting one battle. It is worth spending time on this battle, because when the children have mastered the medium they will be better able to create the effects they want when they come to use the skill in a painting.

Having the right containers and setting out the 'painting station' in a user-friendly way makes a world of difference. Teachers often think that powder paint makes more mess and work than ready-mixed paint but it does not. Indeed, while dry powder does have its difficulties, if it is controlled through good classroom organization, it is less messy than ready-mixed paint and certainly less wasteful.

What is powder paint? An explanation that can be read to children

All paint consists of a colour, and some kind of binding agent which holds it together and makes it stick to the paper or canvas.

In the case of powder paint, the colour has not yet been mixed with a binding agent. That has to be done by the artist, who in this case is you. The binding agent is water. So, when you add water to powder paint, you are in fact mixing your own paint.

Organization of paint and equipment

For all colour mixing activities, only six colours are necessary. These colours are:

❋ Two reds – vermilion and crimson
❋ Two blues – brilliant blue (ultramarine) and cyan (sometimes known as sky blue; it is a turquoisey blue)
❋ Two yellows – brilliant yellow (egg yellow) and lemon yellow.

These can be stored in six plastic paint wells that fit into a small tray and can be placed on the table. The advantage is that you can remove or change the selection of colours if you want to. Black and white are also useful as they cannot be created by mixing, although it is a good idea to dispense a little at a time as a little goes a long way.

The paint wells can be refilled from larger powder paint containers, and the easiest way to do this is to use the paint well like a scoop and dip it directly into the container. Only the most trustworthy of art monitors can be entrusted with this task!

Equipment needed for powder painting

❋ Newspaper
❋ Paper for artwork
❋ One set of paint wells between two children
❋ One water pot between two
❋ One palette between two
❋ Paint, water and palettes need to be positioned so that children do not have to reach across each other to get to them. This causes water and paint to land on their paintings when it shouldn't. See diagram on page 19
❋ A test paper for each child to try out colours and dab their brush on
❋ A pencil, for writing the child's name on the back of work, if nothing else
❋ At least one brush per child; but a selection of brushes of different sizes is better to give children the opportunity to exercise choice.

Key skills in handling powder paint

❋ Controlling the amount of water on the brush and in the palette
❋ Getting the consistency of the paint right
❋ Mixing up enough of the colour
❋ Adding enough pigment
❋ Re-mixing the colour when necessary
❋ Transferring powder to the palette on a brush.

These skills are covered in the powder paint handling lesson on page 29. Children need to revisit this activity at least once a year. Other skills will be covered in colour mixing lessons, such as adding a little of a colour at a time to change a colour/shade.

Tips about using palettes

This is really just common sense, but it is surprising how often children need to have this explained to them.

Things to remind the children about include:

❋ Remember you are sharing the palette; decide with your partner which areas on/in the palette you will each have.

❋ Don't use every part of your palette straight off. Use the space sensibly.

❋ Don't come up and wash your palette every five minutes – it is a waste of paint and a waste of time.

❋ If all your spaces are full, look to see if you can re-use one area again. For example, if you want a brown but there is no space free, then if you have a red mixed up, you can add green to it to make your brown – or, if there is a green mixed up, you can add red to that to get brown. Similarly, if you want a purple and you have a blue mixed, then add red to it, and so on. You don't necessarily need to mix the colour from scratch.

❋ If you do wash your palette, dry it thoroughly or the excess water will make all your new colours too watery.

❋ Washed palettes are better dried with a damp J-cloth than a paper towel. Paper towels are not absorbent enough for the job, and anyway, it is a waste of paper.

❋ When you wash your palette, don't turn the water on full blast and hold the palette under it or you will be sprayed with water. Always angle the palette so that the dirty water runs down into the sink, not down you.

There are other important skills when painting, but these apply to many different painting media, not just powder paint: for example, knowing when to change the water; looking after the brushes. Those aspects will need reinforcing at the beginning of most painting lessons.

Pitfalls of powder paint

❋ It is difficult for children to mix a large amount of a colour. If they need a lot of paint, perhaps for a group or large-scale activity, then ready-mixed paint is more appropriate.

❋ It is hard to re-mix the same colour when it has run out and it will run out quickly. Children need to try to remember how they mixed their colour so that they can achieve that shade again, particularly with browns.

❋ Children will need to be careful transferring paint to the palette from the paint wells. They tend to try to balance precarious heaps of dry powder that can be knocked, sprayed and, more disastrously still, will change the colour too drastically. They need to be reminded that it is best to change a shade or colour gradually with small amounts at a time.

❋ If you are mixing a lot of paint, the powder can tend to float on the surface of the water and be tricky to mix in. This is particularly true of black and the metallic powder paints. A drop of washing-up liquid in the water solves this.

❋ The colours look lovely and bright when just painted, but they lose a little of this brightness when dry.

Joshua Derbyshire, Year 4

Investigating paintbrushes and making different brush strokes

Time 1 hour **Resources** Newspaper to cover tables Per group of 5 or 6 children: Piles of brushes in as many different sizes, shaped ends and lengths of handle as you have in school 2 or 3 paint colours (could be any paint except watercolours) 2 water pots 1 palette For each child: A3 piece of paper For the teacher: One of each type of brush to show A2 piece of paper to demonstrate the brush marks Something to fix paper to board Brush information on page 13 National Curriculum 2a, 4a

Ivy-May White, Year 3

Introduction

Artists use many different types of brushes, depending on what kind of paint they are using, how big or how small the painting is and what kind of effect they want to make. Today you will be looking at the different types of paintbrush and making as many different marks as you can with each type.

Practical activity

❋ Put a big pile of different brushes in front of each group of children and ask them to sort them into piles according to size, handle and end shapes.

❋ Point out that the bristle ends of the brushes may be different lengths and different shapes, and can be made of different kinds of hair.

❋ Ask the children to look for any indication on the brush handles as to the size.

❋ When the brushes have been sorted, explain that different brushes are used for different purposes and will make different marks.

❋ Explain that the metal part of the brush is called the ferrule and that the bristles/hair can be made from different materials, some natural and some man-made (see brush information on pages 13–14).

❋ Tell the children that they should hold the brushes as they would hold a pencil. The best place to hold a brush is just above where the ferrule meets the handle (see Potential pitfall below).

❋ Ask them to mix a slightly thinned solution of paint, then take a short-handled, small soft brush and paint some straight lines and some wavy lines on the paper. Now ask them to repeat this, but press the brush down a little so the lines are wider. Demonstrate.

❋ They could try painting tiny dots, big blobs, flicks and brush strokes of different lengths and thicknesses. Demonstrate.

❋ Encourage them to make as many different marks as they can.

❋ They should now repeat the process with different sizes and types of brush; they could record the size and type of the brush.

Potential pitfall

Children often hold the brush handles either very close to the bristles and get paint all over their fingers which then transfers itself to the painting, or they hold them too far along the handle which makes it difficult for them to control the brush.

Making different brush strokes in a painting

Time
30 min

Resources
Newspaper to cover tables

Per group of 5 or 6 children:
2 or 3 paint colours (could be any paint except watercolours)
Collection of brushes of different types and different sizes
2 water pots
2 palettes

For each child:
A4 piece of black paper

For the teacher:
One of each type of brush to show
A2 piece of paper to demonstrate the brush marks
Something to fix paper to board

National Curriculum
2a, 4a, 5a

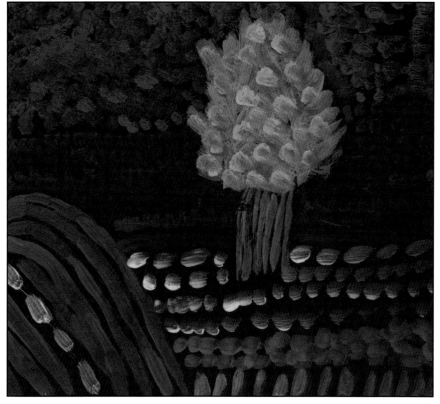

Helen Elmer, Year 4

Introduction
You have tried out making marks with different sizes and kinds of brush, and now you can paint a picture using those brushes. It doesn't matter what you paint (or the subject might be topic led), but what does matter is that you try to make as many different brush strokes and use as many different types and sizes of brush as you can.

Practical activity
* Go over the types, shapes and sizes of brushes if necessary (brush information is on pages 13–14).
* Ask the children to take note of the number on the brush handles which shows the size, and also to notice the different sizes, types and shapes of the bristles.
* Remind the children to hold the brushes as they would hold a pencil. The best place to hold a brush is just above where the metal bit (the ferrule) meets the handle. However, they could try holding the brush handle in different positions, eg at the end of the handle, halfway down, and with their arm fully extended, to see what difference it makes and which they prefer.
* Go over the different brush strokes they could make. Demonstrate tiny dots, long

lines, thick lines, thin lines, zigzags, big blobs and brush strokes of different lengths and thicknesses.
* Extend this by telling them that they can work quickly or slowly, use the brush in different directions, press hard or gently, use the tip, side or edge of the brush, or roll or splay the bristles.
* Encourage them to make as many different marks as they can in their paintings.

Care of brushes
Explain to the children that:
* Brushes should always be washed at the end of a session.
* Watercolour brushes or very dirty brushes can be washed in warm soapy water.
* The ends of watercolour brushes should be shaped back into a point with the fingers after washing.
* Never leave watercolour or soft-bristled brushes ends down in the water pot when not in use. Lay them flat on the table.
* Brushes should always be stored ends downward or flat in a tray, never bristles downward.

Powder paint handling

KEY SKILL

Time
30 min

Resources
Newspaper
Full set of powder paint colours: 2 reds, 2 blues, 2 yellows and black (see page 25)
Water pots
Palettes
Medium long-handled brushes
Cartridge paper
Sketchbooks
Test papers

National Curriculum
2a, 4a

Year 4 pupil

Introduction
Today you are going to be learning (or revisiting) how to handle powder paint. We will be practising how to mix the paint to the right consistency, how to use your palettes, when to change your water and how to get the best out of the colours.

Practical activity
* The lesson could be started by reading the information about powder paint at the start of this chapter (page 25).
* Explain that when the children are mixing up paint it is better not to use a delicate brush. They should use a medium, long-handled brush.
* Remind them to hold the brush just above the ferrule (metal bit).
* Demonstrate the following procedure:
    1. Dip the brush in the water.
    2. Stroke the brush on the top of the water pot to remove surplus water.
    3. Dip the brush into powder colour and transfer to the mixing palette.
    4. Stir the brush around until the powder and water are blended.
    5. Repeat the process until enough paint is mixed for the children's needs.
    6. Test the colour on test paper with just a few dabs or lines of paint.
* Explain that too much water makes the paint very thin and runny and that the consistency should be like cream rather than milk. If the colour is mixed to the creamy consistency then the colour will be as bright and strong as it will go – the crimson will be a deep strong

crimson, the cyan will be a deep strong cyan, and so on; the colour will show its full 'value'.
* Ask the children to experiment with the consistency of the paint and to see how strong they can make a colour.
* Tell the children that if they can see the bottom of the palette through the paint then they have not mixed up enough to paint a strong colour, so they should add more powdered colour to it.
* Suggest children repeat this process with all six of the colours and then the black.
* Next mix an orange, a green and a purple. Tell the children to do this by adding powder paint into an existing mixed colour in their palette, rather than by using a new area of the palette. For example, if they want orange, add a red to a yellow or a yellow to a red. This is good practice for future painting sessions and will reduce the queue at the sink to wash palettes.
* Explain that they should wash their brushes between colours, always wiping the brush on the top edge of the water pot afterwards to control the amount of water going into the paint mixture.
* Water should be changed when it is dirty. Tell the children that they can test if the water needs changing by putting a cleaned brush in the water and dabbing a few watery marks on their test paper. If the dabs are not coloured, then the water doesn't need changing.

Naming paint colours

Time
20 min
Resources
Newspaper to cover tables
Per pair of children:
6 powder paint or ready-mixed colours:
• 2 reds: vermilion and crimson
• 2 blues: brilliant blue and cyan
• 2 yellows: brilliant and lemon yellow
1 water pot
1 palette
For each child:
1 medium long-handled brush
Sketchbooks
For the teacher:
An A2 piece of paper to demonstrate the colours
Masking tape
Colour wheel from page 55 to show
National Curriculum
2a, 4a

Year 4 pupil

Introduction

Paint colours have names. You need to learn six of these names and get used to using them. You might remember them from when you were in your last class. When artists go into an art shop to buy a colour, they will say exactly which colour they want by name, as there are many different shades of every colour. You just need to remember the names of two blues, two reds and two yellows. Does anyone remember any of the names of the six colours you can see in front of you?

Practical activity

❋ Suggest that the children look first at the two yellows and notice the difference. Ask them how they would describe the yellows and in what way they are different. You could tell them that the brilliant yellow is slightly darker and a little closer to orange on the colour wheel, while the lemon yellow is paler and nearer to green. You could also show them a colour wheel from page 55.

❋ Tell them the darker yellow is called 'Brilliant Yellow' and that it is a bit like the colour of an egg yolk.
  • Ask the children to paint a patch of brilliant yellow in their sketchbooks and label it 'Brilliant Yellow'.

• Demonstrate by painting a patch of brilliant yellow paint on the large piece of paper and writing 'Brilliant Yellow' next to it. Tape the paper to the board with masking tape.

❋ Explain that the other lighter yellow is called 'Lemon Yellow'.

❋ Repeat the above steps but using lemon yellow.

❋ Repeat this process with the two reds, explaining that the deeper red is called 'Crimson' and the lighter, more orangey red is called 'Vermilion'. Ask the children to notice the difference between the two colours. Explain that crimson has a touch of blue in it and so is nearer to purple on the colour wheel, while vermilion has a touch of yellow and so is nearer to orange.

❋ Repeat steps shown for brilliant yellow but using each of the two reds.

❋ Explain that the darker blue is called 'Brilliant Blue' and the lighter blue is called 'Cyan'. Cyan has a touch of yellow and so is nearer to green on the colour wheel, while brilliant blue has a touch of red and so is closer to purple.

❋ Repeat steps shown for brilliant yellow but using both blues.

❋ Run over the names of the colours at the end of the session. The children will need reminding of these colour names almost every time they paint. It seems to take a long time to sink in, perhaps because they do not use these names in any other context.

USING SKILL

Painting a picture in powder paint

Time 1 hour **Resources** Newspaper Per pair of children: Full set of powder paint colours (2 reds, 2 blues, 2 yellows – see page 25) Water pots Palettes 1 medium long-handled brushes Fine brushes Cartridge paper Test papers For the teacher: If possible, a copy of Paul Klee's painting, 'Senecio' (1922) Information about Paul Klee on page 95 **National Curriculum** 2a, 4a,c, 5a

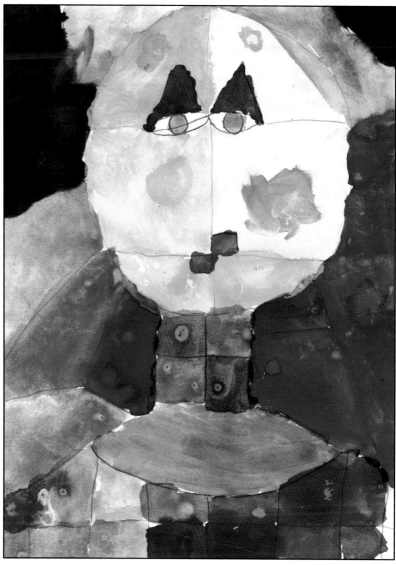

Hannah Roberts, Year 3

Introduction
*You have been developing your skills in handling powder paint
and painting in strong colours. Today you are going to try to use
those skills in a painting.*

*I don't want you to worry about planning a picture; we are
going to borrow the composition from a painting by the Swiss
artist, Paul Klee. Paul Klee loved children's pictures, so I don't
think he would have minded us copying him.*

Practical activity
* Show children a copy of Paul Klee's painting.
  Discuss the colours and shapes.
* Tell the children to draw a large circle on their
  paper which fills most of the page.
* Add a neck and a shoulder line.
* Divide the face in half vertically, and
  approximately in thirds horizontally.
* Next, draw in almond-shaped eyes with

a circular iris, and some small squares to
represent the mouth.
* The neck, shoulder and background can also
  be divided into squares.
* Remind children of steps 1–6 from 'Powder
  paint handling' on page 29.
* Ask them to paint in the face and background
  shapes and aim to paint the colours as
  strong as they will go, giving them their full
  'value'.
* Suggest that they make the background
  colours different colours from the face. For
  example, if the face is mainly oranges, the
  background could be mainly blues, or if the
  face is mainly yellows, the background could
  be purples.
* Tell them to make sure the irises really stand
  out as they do in the original painting.

Getting to know the colours and comparing reds (or blues or yellows)

USING SKILL

Time
30 min

Resources
Newspaper to cover tables

Per pair of children:
6 powder paint or ready-mixed colours:
- 2 reds: vermilion and crimson
- 2 blues: brilliant blue and cyan
- 2 yellows: brilliant and lemon yellow
1 water pot
1 palette

For each child:
1 medium long-handled brush
A3 cartridge paper
Test papers

For the teacher:
A2 piece of paper to demonstrate the colours
Masking tape

National Curriculum
2a, 4a

Chris Nichols, Year 4

Introduction
Today we are going to look at and paint in the two different reds, and you are going to mix some new reds.

Practical activity
* Put the two different reds in front of the children and discuss how they are different.
* Remind children of the names of the reds.
* Revise how to dip the brush in the water and stroke it on the side of the pot to remove the excess water.
* Demonstrate painting a patch of one of the reds on the A2 paper and write the name of the red next to it. Tape this to the board.
* Ask the children to paint a little dab of this colour on their test papers.
* Repeat this with the other red.
* Next, demonstrate transferring a little of one red into the palette and adding a little of the second red to it, then mixing the two reds

together. Paint a patch of this on the A2 paper for the children to see.
* Tell the children to do the same and paint a dab on their test papers.
* Next, give each child a piece of cartridge paper and ask them to cover it with squares and rectangles of as many different reds as then can mix.
* Remind them to try out the colours on their test papers first.
* When the paint is dry, the children could paint patterns over the reds in contrasting reds, eg crimson over vermilion and vice versa.
* This whole activity can be repeated with the two blues and two yellows. When placed on the wall together, they make an attractive display and the labelling can reinforce the names of the colours.

Making a colour lighter without using white (changing tone in colour)

KEY SKILL

Time
20 min

Resources
Newspaper to cover tables

Per pair of children:
Powder paint or ready-mixed colours
– any strong colour
1 water pot
1 palette

For each child:
1 long-handled brush
A5 cartridge paper or sketchbooks
Test paper

For teacher:
An A2 piece of paper to demonstrate
the colours
Masking tape to fix it to the board

National Curriculum
2a, 4a

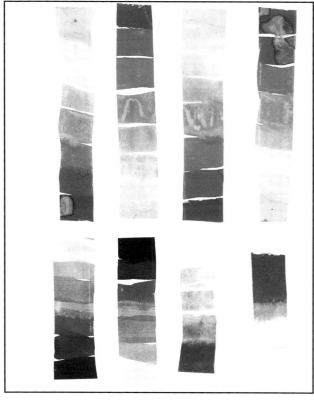

Year 3 pupil (painting has been cut into strips)

Introduction

Today you are going to learn how to make colours lighter. One way is to add white paint, but this can make the colours seem a bit chalky or dull. The other way to make a colour a lighter tone, without using white, is to use more water and less paint. This allows the white of the paper to shine through the paint and it is this that gives it its lightness.

Today you are going to practise this; it is a very useful skill and one that can be used with other types of paint. It is particularly important when you are using watercolours.

Practical activity

❋ Ask the children to mix up whichever colour has been chosen for this exercise. For the purposes of this lesson, we will assume cyan blue. Brilliant blue, crimson and vermilion would also be good choices.

❋ If the children are using powder paint, remind them that the paint needs to be at least the consistency of cream if it is to give its full value.

❋ Next, the children should make a dab of paint on the test paper to check that the cyan is as strong and deep as it will go. Demonstrate just how strong the colour can be.

❋ Now tell them to paint a short broad line in the strongest, deepest tone of cyan across the top of their paper.

❋ Next, ask the children to wash their brushes, then dab their wet brushes in the paint mixture and then try out a dab on their test papers to see what happens when they use a little less paint and a little more water. The cyan should come out a slightly lighter tone. Tell them that they can control the proportion of paint (pigment) to water to vary the tone. Demonstrate this.

❋ Explain that they will need to control the amount of water so that the paint is a light tone but not too runny. This might require some practice.

❋ When they have experimented a little on their test papers, ask them to paint a line of slightly lighter cyan just beneath the first and darkest line.

❋ Next, they should paint a slightly lighter cyan line below that, and so on down the page. Older or more able children could be challenged to make at least seven tones in cyan, while less able or younger children might aim for four tones.

USING SKILL

Painting in one colour and making that colour lighter without using white (changing tone in colour)

Time
30 min

Resources
Newspaper to cover tables

Per pair of children:
Powder paint or ready-mixed colours
– any strong colour
1 water pot
1 palette

For each child:
1 long-handled brush
1 medium/fine short-handled brush
A4 cartridge paper or sketchbooks
Test paper

National Curriculum
2a, 4a, 5a

Beth Wilson, Year 3

Introduction
You have been practising making colours lighter by varying the proportions of water and paint. Now you are going to use this skill in a painting. Try to use as many tones of the same colour as you can. You might wonder what I mean by 'tone' in colour. All colours have a tone. If you look at a black and white photocopy of a coloured picture, you will see that it is made up of different shades of grey and black. These show the different tones (lightness and darkness) that the colours had.

Practical activity
* Ask the children to mix up whichever (single) colour has been chosen for this exercise.
* Ask them to think of a subject to paint.
* Next, ask them to think about which areas of the picture will need to be the deepest tone and which the lightest, and to have this in their minds as they paint. Point out that they cannot make the paint lighter by adding white, so they must be careful about putting on too much paint in the first place.
* Next, children should use their fine brushes, dipped in a pale mixture of their colour, to

sketch out their picture in a very pale tone of their colour.
* If children are using powder paint, remind them that the paint needs to be at least the consistency of cream if it is to give its full value and to always test out their colour on their test papers before using it.
* Encourage the children to start working in a light tone, to add the medium tones as they go along and to finish with the deepest tones. Detail can be added by painting in a deep tone over a medium or lighter one.
* Challenge them to leave little or no white paper showing.

Potential pitfall
Children may well sketch out their composition in a deep tone of their colour unless they are guided not to. If they use a deep tone first, they will end up with dark lines around everything which they will not be able to remove or disguise easily.

Colour mixing

Year 3 pupil

Mixing colours

Crucial to the teaching of painting is recognition that the careful matching, mixing and application of colour requires time.

Mixing and using paint needs much time for the preparation and for introductory activities – so much so that at the end of the allotted time, there may be little to show other than a mass of apparently meaningless splodges of colour and marks. However, the time spent on such activities is never wasted. It provides children with invaluable information to store in their visual memory, so that when they are engaged in a painting activity they have some reference on which to draw.

Colour mixing is one of the most significant aspects in learning how to use paint, and it invites children to discriminate between many qualities of shade and tint. Suddenly their paintings will come alive as this full range of colour is at their disposal. Myriads of colours can be mixed from the three primaries, red, blue and yellow. Children are often amazed at the seemingly endless possibilities.

The skill of mixing paint will require development over a number of years. There is a great deal to learn, and each stage needs to be carefully developed and built on in the future.

Maddie Muirhead, Year 4

Children's descriptive language of colour can be developed side by side with the skills of colour mixing, and they should be encouraged to have a personal response to colour and start to be able to relate it to mood and atmosphere.

If colour mixing is not being prioritized, the many liquid ready-mixed paints that are now on the market are an easy-to-use alternative to powder paint, though it is worth pointing out that these liquid paints may comprise only basic powder colours mixed with water and a thickener. When their cost is considered, this might make them seem an expensive convenience.

Even when using ready-mixed colours, it is still important to encourage colour mixing. To always provide a brush in each pot of ready-mixed colour is to deny pupils a learning opportunity.

Paint provides the best and most flexible medium for exploring colour. For general painting, powder paints give children the best opportunity to do this effectively – but ultimately this is a matter of personal choice by the teacher, and the principles of colour mixing will hold good for all types of paint.

Colour mixing and exploration in acrylics and watercolours are covered in chapters specific to these media later in this book.

Mixing their own colours will help children to develop an awareness and appreciation of colour, and that is a life-enhancing ability which should not be undervalued.

Colour mixing tips
* Crimson is the best red for mixing purples.
* Vermilion is the best red for mixing oranges.
* Cyan and lemon yellow make vivid greens.
* Brilliant blue (ultramarine) and brilliant yellow make natural greens.
* Black and yellow make olive greens.

Black:
* Brilliant blue, crimson, vermilion and brilliant yellow make a near black.
* A pure black cannot be mixed.
* Black added to colours darkens colours but also dulls them.

White:
* White lightens colours but can also dull them.
* Touches of other colours added to white will make different types of white.

Brown:
* Different combinations of the three primaries make different browns.
* Green and red make brown.
* Vermilion and blue make a kind of brown.
* Yellow and purple make a grey/brown.

Skin tones: (all need slight adjustments to match)
* A little of crimson or vermilion with a lot of white and a touch of yellow and the teeniest touch of blue will make a pale skin tone.

* Warm brown and some white make a darker skin tone. Small touches of other colours will vary the shade.
* Cream can be made with white and brilliant yellow and a touch of red.
* Crimson and white make good pinks but not good skin tones.

Note: Colour mixing with watercolour colours is covered in the Watercolours chapter on page 72, because some of the watercolour colours have different names and also there is an extended range of colours to work with.

Sam Warren, Year 4

Mixing secondary colours: oranges (or greens or purples)

KEY SKILL

Time
45 min

Resources
Newspaper to cover tables

Per pair of children:
Powder paint or ready-mixed colours:
- crimson + brilliant blue (for the best purples)
- cyan + lemon yellow (for the brightest greens)
- brilliant yellow + vermilion (for the most vivid oranges)
1 water pot
1 palette

For each child:
1 medium long-handled brush
Cartridge paper
Test paper
Permanent pen

For the teacher:
A3 piece of paper to demonstrate the colours
Masking tape

National Curriculum
2a, 4a

Joe Blackford, Year 3

Introduction
Today we are going to mix orange (or purple or green) for ourselves. We are not going to use orange made up for us already, we are going to make our own oranges. Orange is a secondary colour and it is made by mixing two primary colours together.

Practical activity
- Ask the children which two primary colours are mixed together to make orange.
- Explain that any yellow and any red will make an orange, but that some reds and yellows make brighter oranges than others.
- Ask them to experiment mixing up different oranges and to paint little dabs of these colours on their test papers. These can be stuck into their sketchbooks as a colour mixing reference and they could annotate them, 'red and yellow makes orange'.
- Remind the children how to dip their brush in the water and stroke the brush on the side of the pot to remove excess water.

- Demonstrate how they can make different oranges, not just by using different reds and yellows but also by using different proportions of red and yellow. Show them how to make a light orange by using more yellow than red, and a deep orange by using more red than yellow. Paint patches of different oranges on A3 paper and tape the paper to the board so they can see.
- Now they can use a very watered-down pale orange to paint an oval in the middle of their cartridge paper.
- Tell them to fill the space behind the oval with patches of as many different oranges as they can. Tell them to try to make strong colours by using plenty of paint and not too much water.
- Next they could fill in the oval with patches of either a different secondary colour or a collection of blues or reds to contrast.
- Variations of this could be: background oranges made with one red and one yellow, and oval made up of oranges with a different red and yellow.
- When the paintings are dry, they could draw over the oval and turn it into a mask or face with permanent ink pens.
- This lesson works equally well for purples and greens. The completed work will make a lovely colourful display.

USING SKILL

Mixing secondary colours

Time
1 hour

Resources
Newspaper to cover tables

Per pair of children:
6 powder paint or ready-mixed colours:
- 2 reds: vermilion and crimson
- 2 blues: brilliant blue and cyan
- 2 yellows: brilliant and lemon yellow
1 water pot
1 palette

For each child:
Their colour mixing work from the lesson on page 38 for reference
A choice of brush sizes
Test paper
Cartridge paper

National Curriculum
2a, 4a, 5a

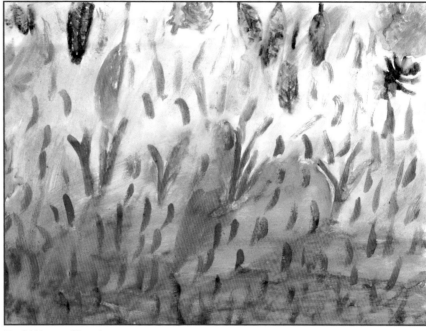

David Young, Year 4

Introduction
You have learned how to mix a wide range of secondary colours – not just one orange using one red and one yellow, but many oranges using combinations of different reds and different yellows. You did the same with greens and purples, and now here is your chance to use as many of those colours as you can in a painting.

Practical activity
❋ Discuss with the children suitable subjects for each of the secondary colours, and put the ideas on the board. The colours do not need to all be in oranges, greens or purples, but should be predominantly in one of those colours.
❋ Possible subjects could be:
  ○ Oranges: sunsets, fires, volcanic eruptions, autumn leaves or still life with flowers and fruit.
  ○ Greens: jungles, forests, gardens, hedges, monsters or still life with foliage, glass bottles and fruit.
  ○ Purples: moorland, flowers, unusual skies, royal costumes, fantastical creatures, eg purple people eater, dragons or wizards.
❋ When the children have chosen their colour and subject, suggest that they draw the composition roughly in a diluted version of their colour, dark enough to be able to see but light enough to change.
❋ Remind them of the range of colours possible by using combinations of different reds, yellows and blues.
❋ Suggest they look at their collections of oranges, greens and purples from the secondary colour mixing lesson.
❋ Explain that they could use the deeper-toned colours as shadows, which are rarely black anyway.

Changing the colours by adding a little paint at a time

Katya Toms, Year 4

Time
1 hour

Resources
Newspaper to cover tables

Per pair of children:
6 powder paint or ready-mixed
colours:
- 2 reds: vermilion and crimson
- 2 blues: brilliant blue and cyan
- 2 yellows: brilliant and lemon yellow
1 water pot
1 palette

For each child:
1 medium long-handled brush
A4 cartridge paper divided into four
sections (see illustration)
Test papers

For the teacher:
A2 paper to demonstrate and tape to
fix to the board

National Curriculum
2a, 4a,b

Introduction

Today you are going to learn a very useful painting skill, one that most painters have to master. It is the skill of changing a colour very, very gradually so you can barely see where the colours change. It a skill that will require some practice, so don't be surprised if at first you find it a bit tricky.

Practical activity

✳ Show the children the illustration above and point out how the colours gradually go from one shade to the next. Tell them this is what they are aiming for.

✳ Ask them first to mix up about a teaspoon of cyan paint in the palette and paint a stripe across the end of one section of the paper. Demonstrate.

✳ Next, tell them to add a tiny amount of lemon yellow to the blue, transferring the paint onto the tip of the brush.

✳ Test the new colour out on the test paper to make sure it is a slightly different colour. If the colour hasn't changed, tell them to add a tiny bit more lemon yellow and test

it out again. Tell the children that they must always test the colour on their test papers before they use it, to compare against the previous colour. This will also help to develop awareness of the subtle differences between colours. If the colour has changed too much, they need to add a bit more cyan back into the mixture. They will need to keep doing this subtle adjusting and comparing of colour throughout the activity.

✳ Now they should paint a stripe of the new colour, which should be just a shade different, right up close so it touches the cyan stripe. Children will need to be careful that their paint is not too watery.

✳ You may need to demonstrate each step.

✳ Next, children should add a little more lemon yellow to the same mixture. They should test the new colour first on the test paper and, if it is just a little different to the last colour made, paint the new colour next to the previous stripe.

✳ They should continue down the paper, aiming to not get to pure lemon yellow before the last stripe.

✳ Older or more able children could be given a longer piece of paper and challenged to not reach yellow before the end.

✳ Now repeat the activity with a cyan and brilliant yellow in the next section, then brilliant blue and lemon yellow in the third section and brilliant blue and brilliant yellow in the last.

✳ This activity can be done with all the reds and yellows, or all the reds and blues.

ACTIVITY

Making a collage using work from the previous lesson

Time
1 hour

Resources
Newspaper to cover tables
Glue sticks
Scissors
A3 paper (could be coloured)
Envelope for each child
Sketchbooks
Pencils

For the teacher:
A2 paper to demonstrate
Blu-Tack®

National Curriculum
2a, 4a,b, 5a

Ellen Corrigan, Year 3

Introduction

We are going to use most of the coloured stripes you painted yesterday to make collages.

Practical activity

❋ Show the children the collage illustrated here (which has been framed with strips from a second colour change combination). Discuss how the colours really show up when they are against a different background, how different dark colours look against light, and how light colours look against dark.

❋ Explain that they are going to make something similar.

❋ Tell the children to cut up their artwork from the previous lesson, along the folds (divisions between each row of colour changes).

| Cyan to Brilliant yellow | Cyan to Lemon yellow | Brilliant blue to Brilliant yellow | Brilliant blue to Lemon yellow |

Colour mixing work cut into four strips

One of these four strips cut into three, with colour changes running down the length of the strip

They will have four strips of different colour changes.

⁂ Ask them to write their names immediately on the back of each strip and put the strips in their envelope as they do so. If this is not done, it will very quickly become impossible for children to tell whose strips of colours are whose.

⁂ Tell the children to take out one strip of colour changes and cut it into three pieces lengthwise.

⁂ Ask them to write their name on two of the strips and put them back in the envelope, and to stick the third strip into their sketch books. They should then label it in their sketchbook, saying which two colours they used.

⁂ Next, repeat that process with the second, third and fourth strips of colour changes, each time cutting each one into three strips, writing their name on two and putting them in their envelopes, then sticking the third piece into their sketchbooks, labelled with the colours used (eg vermilion and brilliant yellow).

⁂ They should now have eight strips of paper with short colour change stripes going across each. There should be two of each kind.

⁂ Lastly, tell the children to lay the strips out on the paper, top to tail (darkest to lightest alternately) and side by side. Demonstrate this by Blu-Tacking a set and fixing it up on the board for the class to see.

⁂ The children can then glue their arrangements down.

⁂ If the children have made more than one set of colours, eg reds to blues or blues to yellows, they can use the other colours to make a multi-coloured collage. These make a stunning display.

The eight remaining strips arranged top to tail (darkest to lightest) alternately

Collage made by sticking strips in different directions

ACTIVITY

Making a collage using work from the previous lesson (easier and an even easier version)

Time
30 min

Resources
Newspaper to cover tables
Glue sticks
Scissors

For each child:
A4 white paper
Sketchbooks
Pencils

For the teacher:
A2 paper to demonstrate
Blu-Tack®

National Curriculum
2a, 4a,b, 5c

Claudia Dixon, Year 4

Introduction

We are going to use most of the coloured stripes you painted yesterday to make collages.

Practical activity

❋ Show the children the collage illustrated here. Discuss how the colours really show up when they are against a different background, how different dark colours look against light, and how light colours look against dark.

❋ Explain that they are going to make something similar.

❋ Tell the children to fold their artwork in half and cut the paper so that they have two sets of colour changes on each piece of paper (Fig. 1).

❋ The children should write their name in the middle of each piece and also write the number 1 on the back of one and the number 2 on the back of the other.

❋ Next they should cut a thin strip (longways) off each outside edge of both piece 1 and piece 2 (Fig. 2).

Crimson to   Crimson to   Vermilion to   Vermilion to
Brilliant yellow   Lemon yellow   Brilliant yellow   Lemon yellow

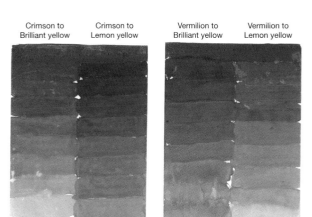

Fig. 1. Colour mixing work cut into two sets of colour changes

Fig. 2. One strip cut off the outside edges of piece 1 and piece 2

* They should now have four thin strips of paper with colour changes all the way down. Children should write their names on these, too (Fig. 3).

Piece 1   Piece 2 cut into 6 strips

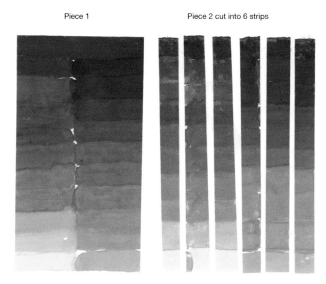

Fig. 4

Fig. 3. Stick all four thin strips into sketchbooks. Label colours, eg Crimson to Lemon yellow

Fig. 5

* Tell them to stick these thin strips into their sketch books. They could annotate them with the names of the primaries they used to make them (eg crimson to lemon yellow, crimson to brilliant yellow, etc).
* Next they should set aside piece 1 and cut up piece 2 into six thin strips, lengthwise so that the colour changes run in steps all the way down (Fig. 4).
* Using the best five strips, children should stick three strips down onto piece 1, with a space in between each. Lastly, stick the remaining two strips either side of piece 1. Strips should run light to dark alternately. (See Fig.5.)

An easier still version
* Cut two or three strips off each colour change set and stick them down in reverse, so light is against dark and dark against light.
* If the children have done more than one set of secondary colours, they could repeat this activity with those. Put together, they make a stunning display.

Recording colour mixing

SKILL

Time
45 min

Resources
Newspaper to cover tables

Per pair of children:
Powder paint or ready-mixed colours:
- crimson + brilliant blue
- cyan + lemon yellow
- brilliant yellow + vermilion
1 water pot
1 palette

For each child:
1 medium long-handled brush
A4 cartridge paper or sketchbook
A pencil
Test paper

For the teacher:
A3 piece of paper to demonstrate the process, and tape to stick it up.

National Curriculum
2a, 4a

$$BB + B\_ = G.$$

$$SB + by = G_2$$

$$SB + ly = G_3$$

Year 3 pupil

Introduction

Today you are going to mix your own colours and record how you made the colours so that you can make them again. Artists often will make their own record of colour mixing for future reference, and that is what you will be doing.

Practical activity

※ Older or more able children will be able to devise their own system for organizing and recording their colour mixing. They need to remember which combinations they have already tried and be able to re-make the colour.

※ Younger children may prefer to use this code and system:
BB for Brilliant Blue
CB or SB for Cyan/Sky Blue
C for Crimson
V for Vermilion
BY for Brilliant Yellow
LY for Lemon Yellow

※ This code could be written on the board and children could copy it into their sketchbooks.

※ Suggest that they start with one colour and

add another to it, for example they could make a green with brilliant blue and brilliant yellow, write: BB + BY = G and then paint a dot of that green. Demonstrate this.

※ Next they could add a little crimson to that green and label it BB + BY + C = G.

※ They could then add a little more crimson to the new colour and label it BB + BY + C + C (or C2) = G and so on.

※ Some children may prefer to write out the names of the colours. This takes a little longer but it works just as well.

※ Children could focus on mixing one range of colours, eg different greens or blues, or they could experiment in making a wide range. They might like to name their new colours (snot green, perhaps? Or perhaps not …).

※ The children could try to recreate their new colours another time, perhaps in the context of a painting (see page 53).

※ Colour recording should be kept for future reference. If the work has not been done in sketchbooks, then it should be stuck in so that children can refer back to it.

Mixing and recording colours: browns

SKILL

Time
45 min

Resources
Newspaper to cover tables

Per pair of children:
Powder paint or ready-mixed colours:
- crimson + brilliant blue
- cyan + lemon yellow
- brilliant yellow + vermilion
1 water pot
1 palette

For each child:
1 medium long-handled brush
A4 cartridge paper or sketchbook
A pencil
Test paper

For the teacher:
A3 piece of paper to demonstrate the
process, and tape to stick it up

National Curriculum
2a, 4a

Year 4 pupil

Note
Cyan can be called 'Sky Blue' or 'Cyan Blue' as 'Cyan' gets confused with 'Crimson' when using a code.

Introduction
Today you are going to mix different browns and record how you made the browns so that you can make them again. Browns are 'tertiary' colours (see page 56) and they are made by mixing the three primaries together in different combinations and proportions. Different blues and reds and yellows combined make different browns, and you are going to investigate and record this.

Practical activity
⁕ Start by writing this code on the board. You may need to put a patch of the colour next to each name in case some children cannot remember the names.
BB for Brilliant Blue
CB or SB for Cyan/Sky Blue
C for Crimson
V for Vermilion
BY for Brilliant Yellow
LY for Lemon Yellow
⁕ The exercise could be organized in different ways, eg different groups of children could investigate different combinations of colours.

⁕ Combinations are:
- Lemon yellow, cyan and vermilion
= LY + CB + V
- Brilliant yellow, cyan and vermilion
= BY + CB + V
- Brilliant yellow, brilliant blue and vermilion
= BY + BB + V
- Lemon yellow, brilliant blue and vermilion
= LY + BB + V
- Lemon yellow, cyan and crimson
= LY + CB + C
- Lemon yellow, brilliant blue and crimson
= LY + BB + C
- Brilliant yellow, cyan and crimson
= BY + CB + C
- Brilliant yellow, brilliant blue and crimson
= BY + BB + C

⁕ Demonstrate how to mix the brown, write the code and paint a dab of brown next to it.
⁕ What they are doing here is mixing different greens and adding red to make brown. Point out to the children that a way to remember how to mix brown is: mix red and green.
⁕ Explain that different proportions of the

three primary colours will give them different browns. For example: one dab of lemon yellow and one dab of cyan and two dabs of vermilion (LY + CB + V + V) will make one brown; two dabs of lemon, one of cyan and one of vermilion (LY + LY + CB + V) will make a different brown.

❋ Tell the children to record their mixing, using their codes, as they go along.

❋ Point out that every brown they make can also be made a lighter or darker tone by using more or less water. The range is enormous.

Year 3 pupil

Year 4 pupil

Mixing and painting in browns

USING SKILL

Time
45 min

Resources
Newspaper to cover tables

Per pair of children:
Powder paint or ready-mixed colours:
• crimson + brilliant blue
• cyan + lemon yellow
• brilliant yellow + vermilion
1 water pot
1 palette

For each child:
1 medium long-handled brush
1 medium-fine short-handled brush
A3 cartridge paper
Previous brown mix recordings
Test paper

National Curriculum
2a, 4a, 5a

Thomas Parkhouse, Year 4 (camouflaged tiger)

Note
Children will need to choose a subject that will give them plenty of scope to use as many different browns as possible, eg mud wrestlers or an autumn scene. In this example, children painted a camouflaged tiger.

Introduction
You are going to re-mix some of those browns you made before and paint a picture using them. Look back at your brown mixing recordings and remind yourself of all the different colours that you made. Try to use as many different browns as you can in your painting and to leave very little background paper showing.

Practical activity
❋ Remind the children of the different ways they can mix browns, and that they can make a brown lighter or darker by using less or more paint than water.
❋ Tell them that whatever subject they choose, they are only allowed to paint in brown, and that they should have little or no white paper left showing.

❋ Tell them they can use green-browns, red-browns, yellow-browns, orange-browns, purple-browns, grey-browns, light browns, dark browns and any other browns they can mix.
❋ These are some points for children to consider before starting their paintings:
  • Where they will start?
  • What will they paint first?
  • Which parts of the painting will be the darkest/lightest?
  • What will be in the background?
  • How big or small will the main items be on the page?
  • Which way up will be the best way to lay the paper?
❋ Tell the children to mix up a brown (any brown will do), then, using a very watered-down version of that brown, lightly outline the main composition.
❋ Now they can start to mix and paint, using whichever browns are best for the subject.
❋ Remind them to look at their colour mixing records to remind themselves of how many browns there are and how to mix them.

Mixing and painting in different whites

USING SKILL

Time
1 hour

Resources
Newspaper to cover tables

Per pair of children:
Powder paint or ready-mixed colours
(ready-mixed white will be easier for
this lesson):
• white
• crimson + brilliant blue
• cyan + lemon yellow
• brilliant yellow + vermilion
1 water pot
1 palette

For each child:
1 medium long-handled brush
A4 cream or pale biscuit-coloured
sugar paper
A pencil
Test papers

For the teacher:
Some paint charts showing a
collection of whites

National Curriculum
2a, 4a, 5a

Wendy Stewart, Year 3

Introduction

*You might be surprised to hear that there is more than one
kind of white. In fact, there are lots of different whites. If any
of your family have been decorating lately and there are paint
charts at home, you will find there are dozens of different
whites and they have fancy names like 'Barley white', 'Pearl
white', 'Moon glow' and so on. You are going to be making
new whites by adding tiny amounts of other colours to white.*

Practical activity

❋ Children should have white paint in several
sections of their palette.
❋ Show the children the paint charts and pass
them around if you have enough. Ask them
to try to work out in what way the whites are
different.
❋ Tell the children to add the tiniest bit of yellow
to white and paint a dab of it on their test
papers. It should be a yellowy-white and not
a pale yellow.
❋ Next ask them to add the tiniest bit of other
colours in turn to clean whites, and test the

results. If they add some secondary colours
and a little water as well as the colours in
the paint pots, they will get a wider range of
whites.
❋ Children should now draw a series of arcs
in the lower two-thirds of the paper, to
represent folding hills.
❋ Next they should paint each section in a
different white, leaving a gap between each
section to represent the shadow between the
hills.
❋ Now children could paint dots of snow in the
sky.
❋ Lastly, they should use pure white to paint
dots of snow across the hills. This will help to
show the difference between pure white and
colour-tinted whites.
❋ If there is time, children could go back
to their test papers and give their whites
different names like those on the paint charts.

Adding black to make a darker colour tone

SKILL

Time
2 hours

Resources
Newspaper to cover tables

Per pair of children:
Powder paint or ready-mixed colours:
• 2 blues: brilliant blue and cyan
• 2 yellows: brilliant and lemon yellow
• 2 reds: vermilion and crimson
• black
1 water pot
1 palette

For each child:
Choice of brush sizes
1 piece of A4 paper or sketchbooks
for recording colours
1 piece of cartridge paper
Test papers

National Curriculum
2a, 4a,b, 5a

Daisy Davies, Year 3

Introduction

All colours have tones. In fact, no two colours have exactly the same tone. The tone of a colour is how light or dark it is. The lightness or darkness of a colour is often a major part of the overall effect of a finished painting. You can create some unusual pictures by considering the tone of your colours as your main focus. You could, for example, paint in mainly dark tones using colours that have a deep tone in the first place, such as purple, violet, brilliant blue (ultramarine), dark brown or deep green. But today you are going to paint a picture using dark-toned colours that you have made yourself by adding black to your colours.

Practical activity

❋ Tell the children that first they are going to practise making darker tones of a colour.

❋ Explain that they will do this adding a very small amount of black at a time.

❋ Suggest that they start with vermilion as it is a mid-tone colour.

❋ Ask the children to mix up some black in their palettes, then paint a dab of black on a piece of paper or in their sketchbooks.

❋ Next tell them to add just enough vermilion to the black to make a slight change from pure black. Test the colour against the black to judge the change. Paint a dab of that colour.

❋ Now add a little more vermilion, check the tone and paint a dab of it.

❋ Continue adding vermilion and recording the new colour until pure vermilion is reached. Now children should have the complete range of tones from black to vermilion. Some children may have ten or more colours while others may manage only four or five, depending on their age, ability and the degree of care taken.

❋ Children could add other colours to black in the same way and record the transition from black to a pure colour and all the tones in between.

❋ Finally, ask them to think of a subject that might look good painted in dark tones and give them a time frame to complete their paintings.

❋ Possible subjects could be: spooky scenes, the woods at night, portraits in sombre lighting and mood, thunderstorms, or even a winter evening.

❋ Remind them to use the best brush for the job, to use their test papers to test the colours and to aim to leave no white spaces.

Creating skin tones

SKILL

Time
30 min

Resources
Newspaper to cover tables/scissors/
glue sticks

Per pair of children:
Powder paint or ready-mixed colours:
- crimson + brilliant blue
- cyan + lemon yellow
- brilliant yellow + vermilion
- white
1 water pot
1 palette

For each child:
1 medium long-handled brush
A4 cartridge paper or sketchbook
A pencil
Test paper
Coloured photographs of faces from
magazines

For the teacher:
A3 piece of paper to demonstrate the
process and tape to stick it up

National Curriculum
2a, 4a, 5a

BY+LY+C+Wh
LY+C+V+BY+Wh
BY+LY+Wh
BY+Wh+V

Year 4 pupil

Note
This activity is more appropriate when the children have covered most of the colour mixing lessons, as it will require all their colour mixing skills. Also, some forethought needs to be given in consideration of vocabulary that will be used to describe different skin colours.

Introduction
Today you are going to mix a range of skin colours. First you will try to mix your own skin colour, and then try to mix the skin colours of people different from yourselves. This will be very useful when you come to paint portraits. You will need to record how you made the colours as you go along, so you can make them again.

Practical activity
* Tell the children that they will need to use a code to record their colour mixing. Tape up a piece of A3 paper, paint a patch of each of the six colours and write the colour name next to it and the code for that colour, eg CR for crimson, SB for sky blue (cyan), etc. This paper could be kept for use on other occasions.

* Go over the following pointers in mixing skin tones and explain that they all need slight adjustments to match:
  - A little of crimson or vermilion with a lot of white and a touch of yellow and the teeniest touch of blue will make a pale skin tone
  - Warm brown and some white make a darker skin tone; small touches of other colours will vary the shade
  - Cream can be made with white and brilliant yellow and a touch of red
  - Crimson and white make good pinks but not good skin tones.

* Demonstrate how to mix at least one of the skin tones and how to record it (eg C + V + W + BY + SB), and show how they can adjust the colour by adding more of one colour or another. Remind them how to make a colour lighter without using white (page 33).

* Ask children to experiment to achieve their own skin tone (they should look at their hands) and to record their colour combinations next to each attempt. At the end, they should put a tick or comment next to the ones they think are the best match.

* Next, ask them to cut a square of skin colour from one of the photographs and stick it on their paper with a good space around it.

* They can then match the skin colours in the photograph, putting dabs of colour next to the square.

* If there is time, they could try to mix other skin tones or try to match hair and eye colours.

USING SKILL

Painting a self-portrait using skin tones

Steve Latham, Year 4

Time
1 hour

Resources
Newspaper to cover tables

Per pair of children:
Powder paint or ready-mixed colours:
- crimson + brilliant blue
- cyan + lemon yellow
- brilliant yellow + vermilion
- white
1 water pot
1 palette

For each child:
A choice of brush sizes
A mirror
A4 cartridge paper or sketchbook
Skin tone mixing recordings from
previous session
HB pencil
Test paper

For the teacher:
A3 piece of paper to demonstrate the
process, and tape to stick it up

National Curriculum
2a, 4a, 5a

Introduction
Today you are going to paint a self-portrait. You will be using the skills of mixing skin tones that you have already practised so you will need to look back at the recordings you made when you mixed those colours.

Practical activity
 The children should have a good, long look at their faces in their mirrors. I usually allow a set time for children to be silly with mirrors – say 5 minutes – to get it out of their system.

❋ They should note face shape, hairline and expression.

❋ Next, they should lightly mark out the overall shape of the head, filling the paper.

❋ Go over these points:
  - Everyone has a neck.
  - Eyes come approximately half way down the face.
  - The hairline, even with very short hair, starts about a fifth of the way down the forehead, not at the top.
  - No detail (eg eyelashes), as this is to be a painting, not a painted drawing.

❋ Explain that the focus is painting the skin tones. Detail can be put in later with a fine brush if there is time.

❋ Then look at their colour mix recordings from the last session.

❋ Ask the children to mix up their skin tone and to paint a light version (less paint, more water) of this colour right across the face and neck of the painting, just leaving eyes and hair unpainted.

❋ Next they should paint another layer of the same colour over the areas where there is shadow, such as the neck beneath the chin, the eye sockets, down the sides of the nose and anywhere else they can see shadows. Tone can be built up in layers in this way. The darkest areas can be added last.

❋ Encourage the children to mix a natural mouth colour, using maybe a blend of the two reds and a touch of brilliant yellow, and then paint the mouth in a watered-down version of this colour, varying the tone to create highlights. No bright red mouths! The lower lip is usually a lighter tone than the upper lip.

❋ Hair and eyes can be painted next, leaving the white paper for the whites of the eyes, and then the background.

❋ Detail, texture and pattern could now be painted with a fine brush.

Using a range of colours in a painting

USING SKILL

Time
45 min

Resources
Newspaper to cover tables

Per pair of children:
Powder paint or ready-mixed colours:
- crimson + brilliant blue
- cyan + lemon yellow
- brilliant yellow + vermilion
- black
1 water pot
1 palette

For each child:
1 medium long-handled brush
1 fine short-handled brush
A4 cartridge paper with a 2cm border
and middle shelf drawn.
A pencil
Test paper

National Curriculum
2a, 4a

Work of five Year 4 pupils, paintings mounted one above the other

Note
This should give children good opportunities to mix and paint with a full range of colours. Here the subject was a bookcase to link in with the Book Week in school. Possible subjects could be: a carnival, flower beds, party costumes, fabrics, etc.

Introduction
You are going to do a painting and try to use a good range of different colours that you have mixed yourself. Don't use any pure unmixed colours straight from the pot/bottle. You could look back in your sketchbooks to see how you made different colours and see if you can re-mix them.

Practical activity
- Ask the children to look at a bookcase in the classroom or the library, noting how the books are different colours and different sizes.
- They could lightly sketch out rectangular book spines of different heights and thicknesses arranged along the shelf.

- Draw their attention to the way some books are leaning at an angle and some have spaces between them.
- Next tell the children to try to paint a shelf of books, painting the spine of each book a different colour.
- When the paintings are dry, children could paint titles, or squiggles to represent titles, and small images along the spines, in different colours. They could look at books in the classroom to get some ideas.
- Draw their attention to the fact that the writing down the spine is often in a different colour. Encourage them to do the same.
- Lastly, they should mix the darkest colour they can and paint the shadows behind the books, or they could use black.
- If the paintings are displayed one above the other they give the impression of a bookcase and make a colourful display.

Colour matching

SKILL

Time
1 hour

Resources
Newspaper to cover tables
Glue sticks
Scissors

Per pair of children:
Powder paint or ready-mixed colours:
• 2 blues: brilliant blue and cyan
• 2 yellows: brilliant and lemon
• 2 reds: vermilion and crimson
• black and white
1 water pot
1 palette

For each child:
1 medium long-handled brush
1 fine brush
Cartridge paper
Test papers
A coloured photograph from a
magazine

National Curriculum
2a, 4a,b,c, 5a

Robert Steel, Year 4 (pupil's colour testing to left)

Introduction

Today you are going to practise something that might be very useful to you in life, whether you become a grown-up artist or not. It is the skill of colour matching. What we mean by colour matching is finding or making a colour that is as near as possible to being the same as another one. The best way to do this is to look at the colour very carefully and try to work out what kind of colour it is that you are trying to match. If it is a brown, for example, you could ask yourself questions like: 'Is it a dark brown or a light brown?' 'Is it a yellowy brown or a brown that has a lot of green in it?' 'How did they make this colour – what colours did they use?' You could call this 'unpacking the colour'. You are trying to work out what other colours have been used in making the colour, in order to make it yourself. You are going to try to match the colours from photographs as near as you possibly can.

Practical activity

❋ Explain to the children that they are going to try to match the colours from photographs, as closely as they can.

❋ Tell them to cut out part of their photograph and stick it in the middle of their paper. The remainder should be hidden away until the end of the session.

❋ The idea is that they should extend the image to fill the paper; they could change or adapt the image, but the colours must continue as near as possible to the ones in the photograph, particularly at the point where the paint touches the photograph.

❋ Children might like to sketch in lightly where and how the image extends.

❋ Remind them to test their own made colours on their test papers and against the photograph. They should hold the test paper, with the dab of mixed paint colour, right next to the colour in the photograph to see if it matches.

❋ Just for interest, at the end of the session, children could get out the remainder of their photograph from where they hid it and see how closely they matched the original image.

Colour theory

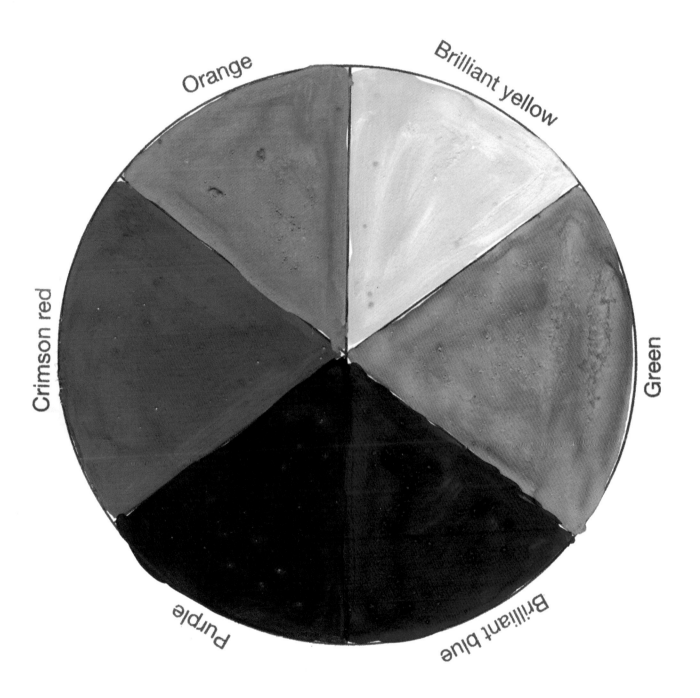

A completed colour wheel

Background information

This background information can be read out to the children

Without light there is no colour. Our main natural source of light is the sun. Colour is not an independent substance on the surface of an object but the reflection of light. Reflected waves of light affect our colour sense.

This is a bit like music and the pitch of sounds; ten vibrations a second means one sound, eleven means another, twelve another, and so on. (There are sound waves and there are also light waves.) In the same way, between light made up of waves running at 400 billion to the second and light made up of waves running at 800 billion to the second, there are hundreds of billions of colours.

The spectrum

If we take white light and pass it through a prism, we get a band of colours called the spectrum.

In the solar spectrum (as seen in the rainbow), the colours are not separate and you cannot tell where one colour ends and the next begins. If you simplify the spectrum by dividing it into bands of all the pure colours, you can bend this band into a circle. This is called a colour wheel.

Primary colours

The three primary colours are red, blue and yellow. They are called primary colours because they cannot be made from any other colours. You cannot make a blue by mixing other colours together. You can make different types of blue by adding other colours to a blue, but you cannot make a blue unless you have a blue in the first place. It is the same for red and yellow.

From these three primary colours we can mix all the rest.

Printers use a red that is a deep pink-red and known as magenta, a turquoise-blue known as cyan and a brilliant yellow. When they use these three colours, they can create every conceivable colour.

Secondary colours

Orange, green and purple are called secondary colours because they are made by mixing two primary colours together.

Blue and red make purple, red and yellow make orange, and blue and yellow make green.

The colour wheel

Colour wheels are a useful way of showing the effects of mixing paints.

The colours always go round the wheel in the same order, but some colour wheels have more colours than others. In the simplest colour wheel, there are six colours: three primaries and three secondaries. The colours are always arranged so that the primary colours are next to a secondary colour and directly opposite a colour that complements it. You could think of complementary colours as 'opposite colours'.

One side of the wheel has colours that look warm (red, orange, yellow) and the other side has colours that look cool (blue, green, purple.)

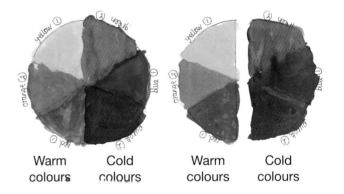

| Warm colours | Cold colours | Warm colours | Cold colours |

Tertiary colours

Tertiary colours are colours created using different combinations of all three primary colours. The different proportions make different colours. If red is the dominant colour, a brown will be made, if yellow dominates, then ochre will be created, and if blue dominates it will be an olive colour.

Complementary colours

Each colour on the colour wheel has a complementary colour which sits opposite it on the wheel. When two complementary colours are put next to each other, they contrast with each other and seem more vivid.

Complementary pairs of colours are red and green, blue and orange, and purple and yellow. If these pairs are mixed in paint, they make a kind of grey-brown.

When colour mixing, if a little of a complementary colour is added to another, it makes a darker tone of that colour. For example, a little purple added to yellow makes a darker yellow. This is useful when painting shadows.

Harmonizing colours

When colours are next or very close to each other on the colour wheel, they are called harmonizing colours because they appear to blend together.

Earth colours

These include browns, greys, blacks, rusty reds and ochre, burnt sienna, raw umber, burnt umber, cinnamon, ginger, etc. Colours in this range are called earth colours.

Hot and cold colours

Pinks, red-dominant purples, reds, yellows, warm browns and oranges are considered warm/hot colours.

Blue-dominant purples, blues, greens, greys and blacks are considered cold colours. Warm colours stand out in a picture and cool colours seem to recede.

Colour moods

Different colours are associated with different feelings, although not everyone feels the same way about colours. These are some feelings generally associated with colours:

* Red = anger, danger, aggression, heat
* Blue = sadness, depression, loneliness, cold
* Yellow = happiness, cowardice, anxiety, jealousy
* Purple = passion, poison, royalty
* Green = envy, inexperience, youth, spring
* White = innocence, cold, winter
* Black = purity, power, death, strength, night time

There are many more, and often the associations are quite contradictory. This is because colour gets different responses from different people, and also because colours have different symbolism in different cultures.

Artists can use colour to create a response in the viewer by drawing on these associations, which are quite powerful and often deep-seated.

How artists use colour theory to create certain effects

If an artist wants to give the illusion that something is near in their picture, or far away, there are two ways they can do this. One is to use scale, but the other is to use colour.

The further away something is supposed to be from the viewer, the smaller it is shown. But if artists want something to appear to be in the far distance of their picture, they could also use cool pale colours, soft blues or very pale purples – misty colours. If, on the other hand, they want something to seem nearer or to stand out, they could use warm strong colours, such as a bright red or vivid orange.

If they want to create a powerful or dramatic effect, they might well use two complementary colours together. If they want a peaceful, calm image, they might use lighter tones of harmonious colours. They can actually break all the rules of colour theory and still create one of these illusions.

Tone in colour

A colour can be made lighter or darker in tone in two ways.

The first way is by adding white gradually. This will make a colour lighter and lighter by degrees. Black can be added in the same way, to make it darker.

The second way is achieved by using less paint and more water. This will make different tones of the same colour, from palest tone to deepest tone. It can be done by varying the proportions of water to paint.

For example, from crimson you could make a very pale delicate pink which you can hardly see, a medium pink or a deep crimson. The white of the paper shines through the colour and acts in the same way as the white paint to make the colour lighter in tone.

This takes more skill and control, but the colour achieved is clearer and less chalky. More pigment and less water makes a deeper and more intense tone of the same colour. It is possible to make many different tones of the same colour this way. Either of these methods could be used for every one of the hundreds of billions of colours, so the possibilities are endless.

Key aspects of colour theory

Primary colours

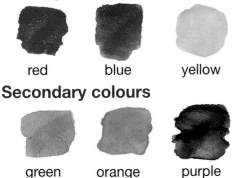

red　　　　blue　　　　yellow

Secondary colours

green　　　orange　　　purple

Tertiary colours

Tertiary colours are made by mixing all three primaries and are mostly variations of brown.

Complementary colours

red + green　　　　blue + orange　　　　yellow + purple

Complementary colours contrast.

Harmonious colours

Harmonious colours are close to each other on the colour wheel. They appear to blend when close to each other.

Earth colours

browns　　black　　greys　　rusty-reds　　orangey-browns

Warm colours

pinks　　red-purples　　reds　　oranges　　yellows　　browns

Warm colours advance (seem closer) in a picture.

Cool colours

blues　　greens　　blue-purples　　greys　　black　　green-yellows

Cool colours recede (seem further away) in a picture.

The colour wheel

KEY SKILL

Time
45 min to 1 hour

Link
Science

Resources
Newspaper
Powder paint in 6 colours:
- 2 reds: vermilion and crimson
- 2 blues: brilliant blue and cyan
- 2 yellows: brilliant and lemon yellow
Water pots
Palettes
Medium and fine brushes
Test papers
Photocopies of resource sheet 1 on page 116
Colour wheel to show (page 55)

National Curriculum
4a

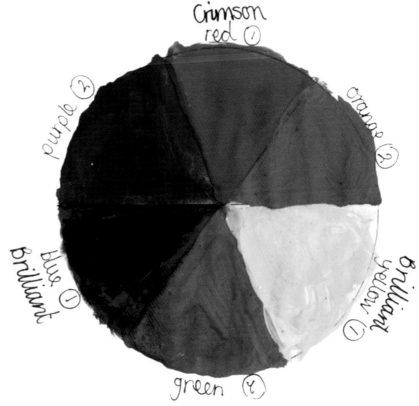

Year 4 pupil

Note
This activity can be done using ready-mixed paint if you have the six colours, but it is much better to use powder paint. If children have never used powder paint before, they need to have a quick session in powder paint handling first (see page 29).

Introduction
Today we are going to make some colour wheels and learn about colour theory and how artists use this to help them to create particular effects. (The information about colour theory on pages 56–58 could be read now, all or in part, to children, but with particular reference to the colour wheel.)

The colour wheel is a diagram that helps us to understand more about colours and how they affect each other. You are going to make two colour wheels, the first one using the orangey red (vermilion), the greeny blue (cyan) and the lemon yellow. You will see the names on your colour wheels.

Practical activity
❊ For younger or less able children, put out only the three colours stated.
❊ Point out that the colours are written on the wheel and that is where they must paint them in, or the wheel will not be correct
❊ Children paint the three primary colours on wheel 1.

❊ Next mix green, purple and orange and paint in the correct sections.
❊ Explain that they are now going to repeat the activity with a different red, blue and yellow to compare the secondary colours created.
❊ Repeat the activity with the other colours – crimson, brilliant blue and brilliant yellow – on colour wheel 2.
❊ Refer back to the colour theory and ask such questions as: 'What colour is complementary to orange/purple/green?' 'Name three warm colours,' 'Name three cold colours.'
❊ Ask questions such as: 'Which red and blue do you think make the best purple?' 'Which blue and yellow make the brightest or most natural green?'
❊ Ask 'What colours would you use if you wanted them to stand out from the other colours or for a poster?' 'Which colours would you use to paint a cold winter's day?'
❊ When dry, the colour wheels should be stuck in the children's sketchbooks for future reference.

Revisiting and extending knowledge of colour theory

KEY SKILL

Time 1 hour **Link** Science **Resources** Newspaper Powder paint in 6 colours: • 2 reds: vermilion and crimson • 2 blues: brilliant blue and cyan • 2 yellows: brilliant and lemon yellow Water pots Palettes Medium and fine brushes Test papers A3 photocopies of resource sheet 2 on page 117 A colour wheel to show (page 55) or colour wheels in their sketchbooks from previous lesson **National Curriculum** 4a	

The colour wheel   Hot colours   Cold colours

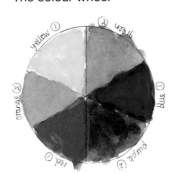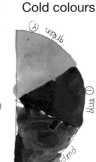

Complementary colours

Harmonious colours
Take any two colours that are next to each other on the colour wheel and make three of each. For example:

3 greens and 3 blues or   3 blues and 3 purples or
3 purples and 3 reds or   3 reds and 3 oranges or
3 oranges and 3 yellows or   3 yellows and 3 greens or …

Year 4 pupil

Note
For younger or less able children, or if it is likely that children might not remember which colours are complementary, harmonious, etc, photocopy the key points from the colour theory background notes on pages 56–58 and ask children to stick them in their sketchbooks. Alternatively, you could write the key points on the board.

Introduction
Today we are going to look at colour wheels to remind ourselves about colour theories and how artists use these theories to help themselves create particular effects in their paintings. We are going to paint a new colour wheel which has a lot more colour information on it. It should be helpful to you when you are creating your own paintings on other occasions.

Practical activity
* Go over the colour theory information (page 56).
* Discuss the various sections of the worksheet and what colours they will put where.
* Ask the children to paint in all the colours on the worksheet. If they forget which colours are primary and secondary, complementary,

harmonious and so on, remind them that the information is on the board or in their sketchbooks.
* Remind the children to try out a little dab of each colour on their test papers to check it is the colour they want – not too pale or dirty from a dirty brush or water.
* Encourage them to change their water when they need to.
* Suggest that they choose to paint a section that is not next to a painted section that is still wet. Ask them why this is (the colours might run).
* Tell the children to try to keep inside the lines and remind them to make sure they have the right sized brush for the job.

Painting using colour theory

USING SKILL

Time
1 hour

Resources
Newspaper
Powder paint in 6 colours or ready-mixed paint if preferred:
- 2 reds: vermilion and crimson
- 2 blues: brilliant blue and cyan
- 2 yellows: brilliant and lemon yellow
Water pots
Palettes
Medium and fine brushes
Cartridge paper
Test papers
Their own extended colour theory resource sheets from the previous lesson

National Curriculum
2a,b, 4a,c

Shona Gregory, Year 4 (hot colours)

Note
The colour theory assessment sheet on page 63 could be done in clearing-up time.

Introduction
Today we are going to test out the colour theory we covered the other day and you can find out if it works.

Practical activity
❋ Ask the children to look at their extended colour theory sheet (from the lesson on page 60).

❋ Read through the sections of colour theory on pages 56–58 relating to complementary, harmonious, hot and cold, earth colours, colour moods and how artists use colour theory.

❋ Discuss with the children and ask for their own ideas about colour moods.

❋ Tell the children that they can choose any one of the following options:
- Paint in all harmonious colours to create a pleasant mood.
- Try to create a cold or hot scene by painting in cool or hot colours.
- Try to paint a landscape and make things in the distance look further away.
- Make something stand out in a painting by using complementary colours.
- Choose one of the colours and try to create a colour mood by painting predominantly in that colour.

❋ Discuss other ideas that the children may have.

❋ Children could choose their own subject matter for the paintings.

❋ Encourage them to cover the whole page, leaving no white background.

❋ When the paintings are complete, hold some up and discuss whether the theory works or not in each of these paintings.

❋ Children could make a note in their sketchbooks about how they feel the theory worked and how they could use it more effectively another time.

Trying out different colour combinations

USING SKILL

Time
1 hour

Resources
Newspaper
Powder paint in 6 colours or ready-mixed paint if preferred:
- 2 reds: vermilion and crimson
- 2 blues: brilliant blue and cyan
- 2 yellows: brilliant and lemon yellow
Water pots
Palettes
Medium and fine brushes
Cartridge paper or squared paper
Test papers
Sketchbooks or scrap paper
Access to Wassily Kandinsky's 'Colour Studies' and Terry Frost's 'October Tambourine'

National Curriculum
2a,b, 4a,c

Ebony Thorn, Year 4

Introduction

We have talked about colour theory and how artists use it to help them create different effects. Today you are going to try out different combinations of colours and notice how they change when they are placed close to other colours. Whether colours 'go' or not is a matter of personal preference, and one person's ideas about colour can be very different from another's. For centuries, artists have played around with colour. Sometimes artists paint solely in coloured shapes, which might look to you like just a lot of coloured squares or circles but the artist's focus has been on how colours behave when they are next to other colours. They would think for a long time about what colours to use and what the effect will be. This is what you are going to do.

Practical activity

* Tell children to try this out on scrap paper or in their sketch books:
  1. Paint three circles or squares of orange (not too close together).
  2. As soon as the colour is dry enough, paint blue around one of the orange shapes, yellow around another and red around the last one.
* Discuss how the orange looks different when it is surrounded by different colours. Repeat this with other colour combinations.
* Show examples of the work of the artists Kandinsky and Frost.
* Suggest that children fold their paper into squares and start by painting a circle of their first colour in the middle of one of the squares.

* Next, they should consider what colour they will paint around it and then what colour the circle around that should be, and finally the rest of the square background behind the circle.
* Children should try using complementary colours together, and sometimes harmonious colours. They should also paint an area of the picture in warm colours and other areas in cool colours.
* They should now fill all the squares, considering which colours seem to jump out and others blend together.
* They now continue to fill the squares, considering at each stage how the overall effect has changed and what colour they might put next.
* This is a slow, considering activity and children do not need to have covered their paper. It is better if they have painted just a few colours, and have thought carefully about them, than they fill in their paper without really responding to the colours and their impact.
* Children could look at their work at the end of the session and think about how they feel about their colours and combinations of colours they have used.
* They could ask themselves questions such as: 'Which colours stand out?' 'Which colours do I like together?' 'Which bit of the painting doesn't seem to "work"?' 'Why do I think this?' These responses are subjective to the child

Assessing knowledge of colour and colour theory

Name   _____

Name the three primary colours   _____

Name the three secondary colours   _____

Which colour is complementary to:

blue   _____

red   _____

yellow   _____

Which two colours make orange?   _____

Which two colours make green?   _____

Which is the best blue and best red for making purple?   _____

_____

Which colours mix together to make brown?   _____

_____

Name two cold colours   _____   _____

Name two warm colours   _____

Name two earth colours   _____

Which colour is thought to be a sad colour?   _____

Which colour is thought to be a happy colour?   _____

Which colour belongs in the gap?   _____ with envy

Which colour belongs in the gap?   _____ for danger

List the colours in the order they come in the spectrum (rainbow) or, if you have coloured pencils or felt tips, draw a rainbow.

_____

_____

Watercolours

Aflie Mathews, Year 3

Introduction to watercolours

Watercolours are made of finely powdered pigments (colours) to which gum has been added to bind them together. The gum dissolves easily in water and helps to fix the colour to the paper. The colours are pure and translucent and can be built up in layers.

A brief history

Many people think that watercolour painting was invented in the 18th century, but in fact it was a fully developed art form long before that. The ancient Egyptians were using watercolours to illustrate their Books of the Dead two thousand years before the birth of Christ. Medieval illustrators were highly skilled in the craft and the earliest of them used 'pure' (meaning 'transparent') watercolour, while later ones added other substances to make the paint more solid and to create a base on which gold leaf was laid.

The British artist JMW Turner (1775–1851) worked a great deal in watercolours and the medium remained popular right through the Victorian era. Edward Hopper (1882–1967) and others continued the tradition in America, while Edward Burra, David Jones and Paul Nash were perhaps the major English exponents. The Swiss artist Paul Klee (1879–1940), a founder member of the Bauhaus, produced his most significant work in the medium.

Character of the medium

The chief characteristics of watercolour paint are its transparency and pureness of colour. The whiteness of the paper shines through and gives the colours light. The paint should be used thinly and the painter must build up the picture, working through from the lightest tones to the darkest. Once a colour has been laid, it cannot be easily lightened. Even a very light tone laid over another colour will darken it further by covering more of the white paper underneath. It is this quality of the paper shining through the transparent pigment that gives pictures in watercolours the sparkle and brilliance that sets them apart from other types of painting.

Mistakes can be difficult to correct. Only delicate colours can be washed out with a clean wet brush or a piece of sponge or cotton wool.

In watercolour, only the paper is white; white paint is generally not used. The artist starts with the most delicate colours and adds by over-painting.

Paint

The paints can be purchased in tablets of colour, powdered or in tubes. The tablets, which come in tins of twelve or so colours, are adequate for most needs in primary school. The powder, which is made up with water and generally known as 'Brusho®', is very useful with all ages. The tubes will work out quite expensive as there will be more waste. However, they could be used for art clubs or small groups of children.

The coloured tablets can be bought separately and the spaces in the tins refilled when necessary. The yellow tends to run out first.

Eli Petch, Year 3

Brushes

Watercolours are best applied with soft flexible brushes. Buy the best brushes you can afford and keep them especially for watercolours or delicate work. A range of sizes is important, including some big, soft brushes for laying washes. The best watercolour brushes have sable hair and are very expensive, but squirrel hair makes a reasonably priced substitute. There is more information about brushes on page 13.

Paper

Watercolours need to be painted on heavier weight paper than is used for general painting. Proper watercolour paper comes in different thicknesses and with different textures. You can buy it from art shops in blocks, spiral-bound pads or as individual sheets. It will be too expensive for most school art budgets, but heavier cartridge paper will do fine. 190 g/sm (90 lb) or above won't wrinkle too much when painted on. Perhaps a block of watercolour paper could be bought for final paintings at the end of a unit of work, and small pieces could be cut up in advance for children to experiment on.

Proper watercolour papers can be 'rough', which has the most texture, 'not' or 'cold-pressed', which has a semi-rough texture, or 'hot-pressed', which has the smoothest surface.

Dry, damp or wet paper

Generally, watercolours are painted on wetted paper. The paper may just be a little damp or it can be quite wet – it depends on the effect desired. The wetter the paper, the looser and freer the effect will be, and colours will blend and blur into each other. Damp paper allows for a bit more control, and dry paper will leave sharp edges which cannot be removed or dried. It is good for children to experiment with these different effects.

Colours

The following twelve colours, which are generally included in most tins supplied to schools, enable children to mix whatever colours they need: Black, Van Dyke brown, Burnt sienna, Carmine (crimson), Vermilion, Prussian blue, Ultramarine, Hooker's green, Leaf green, Yellow ochre, Gamboge (brilliant yellow), White (although it is not often used, it generally comes in the tin).

Useful additions are: Lemon yellow, Raw umber, Payne's grey and Cerulean blue.

I would not recommend the use of masking fluid, as children can have an allergic reaction to it. I had it happen once in a class and I have never used it since.

Year 5 pupil (varying colour tones)

SKILL Getting to know the colours and the box layout

Time
30 min

Resources
Per pair of children:
1 box of watercolour paints
1 water pot

For each child:
1 medium-fine watercolour brush
A pencil
Copy of resource sheet 3 (on page 118) or sketchbook

For the teacher:
1 tin of watercolours to show

National Curriculum
2a,c, 4a

Introduction
Today we are going to get to know the colours in the watercolour box. The names are a little different from the names of powder and ready-mixed paint. In the tin, some of the colours look very dark, and you might be surprised when you try them to find that they are a dark blue, a dark green or a dark brown.

Before the activity
* Show the tin of watercolours and read out the names of the colours.
* Tell the children that the names of the colours are similar to the names of oil paint colours, and that paint colours are often named after the plant, rock, earth, animal or place they originally come from. However, most paints are made from chemicals now.
* Tell them that the two reds are similar to the reds in powder paint.
* Explain that:
  * Prussian blue is very different from cyan. Prussian blue is a dark greeny-blue which, when mixed with burnt sienna, makes some lovely browns. Prussia is a country that no longer exists (it is now part of Germany).
  * Ultramarine is a blue paint that used to be made from a semi-precious stone called lapis lazuli. It used to be incredibly expensive and only rich patrons could afford to buy it for their painters, but the colour is so good that paintings painted with it 500 years ago are as bright today as they were when they were painted. Ultramarine literally means 'beyond sea' (which is where lapis lazuli was imported from).

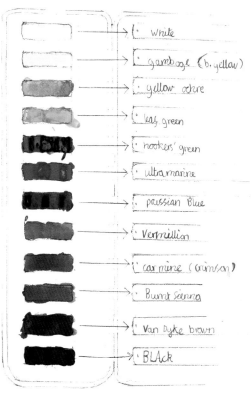

Nicky Loat, Year 3

* Raw sienna is an earth colour made from a natural clay containing iron (originally found in Siena, Italy), and burnt sienna is raw sienna that has been roasted in a furnace.
* Yellow ochre is an earth-colour made from clay containing iron.
* Gamboge is a gum resin made from various Asian trees. It was once used as a cure for constipation. (They will like that!)
* Hooker's green is named after the English painter, W Hooker, who first used it.
* Vandyke brown is named after the Dutch artist Anthony Van Dyck.
* Tell them that they will rarely use the white.

Practical activity
* Ask the children to miss the first space and to paint gamboge in the space below and then write the name of the colour next to it. Tell them to paint the colour as strong as it will go.
* Write the name of each colour in turn on the board for the children to copy.
* Next they should paint yellow ochre, then leaf green and so on, in the same order as they come in the tin. The order may vary according to the manufacturer.
* The completed sheets should be stuck in the children's sketchbooks for future reference.

How to use watercolours and how to make lighter colours without using white

SKILL

Time
30 min

Resources
Per pair of children:
1 box of watercolour paints
1 water pot
Small palette if required
(not really necessary as the lid will do)

For each child:
1 medium watercolour brush
A paper towel
A4 cartridge paper or sketchbook

For the teacher:
1 tin of watercolours to show
Paper to demonstrate

National Curriculum
2a,c, 4a

Year 4 pupil

Note
This lesson can be combined with either the previous one or the one that follows and done in the same session.

Introduction
In watercolour painting, you rarely need to use the white. Lighter colours can be made by using less paint and more water. You don't need white because the white of the paper shines through the paint and gives the colours their lightness. You are going to try to make a full range of tones for each colour from a deep tone, all the way to the very palest tone of that colour. It is a very, very useful skill and one you will be able to use when you are painting.

Practical activity
❋ Demonstrate how to use the medium:
  1. Wet the brush and blot it on a paper towel to remove excess water.
  2. Move the brush to and fro over the colour until the bristles are covered in paint.
  3. Dab the paint onto the lid of the tin or a palette and repeat until there is enough paint for purposes (for this activity, colours can be used straight from the tin).
  4. Then paint with colour.

❋ Tell the children not to scrub with the brushes as they will ruin them, and not to leave the brushes standing bristle-end down in the water but always to rinse them and lay them down flat on the table.

❋ Next, demonstrate how to make the colour go lighter and lighter until you have a pale tone you can barely see.

❋ Repeat steps 1 and 2 above and then paint a patch of colour.

❋ Immediately wash the brush, put the wet brush into the patch of colour and pull the colour away from the patch a few centimetres.

❋ Wash the brush again, put it back on to the place where you left off and pull the colour a few centimetres further away still. Keep repeating this until there is no colour left.

❋ This is quite a tricky technique, and one that will need a bit of practice. Tell the children that they will have to move fast so that the colour does not dry. Once it is dry, it will have dyed the paper and the colour will not easily be removed.

❋ Allow them time to experiment and to try it out with a range of colours. The water will need changing often.

Painting in lighter and darker tones of colour

USING SKILL

Time
1 hour

Resources
Per pair of children:
1 box of watercolour paints
1 water pot
Small palette if required (not really necessary as the lid will do)

For each child:
1 medium watercolour brush
1 fine brush
A paper towel
A4 cartridge paper or sketchbook

For the teacher:
Paper to demonstrate

National Curriculum
2a,c, 4a

Tabitha Waldron, Year 3 (Devon hills)

Note
This lesson can be combined with the lesson on page 68 and done in the same session.

Introduction
In watercolour painting, you rarely need to use the white. You don't need white because the white of the paper shines through the paint and gives the colours their lightness. Lighter colours can be made by using less paint and more water. You are going to try paint a picture entirely in one colour and you will have to think carefully about which parts of your picture need to be dark and which light, before you start.

Practical activity
※ Revise how to use the medium.
※ Tell the children not to scrub with their brushes as they will ruin them, and not to leave them standing hair-end down in the water but always to rinse them and lay them down flat on the table.
※ Next, demonstrate how to make the colour go lighter and lighter to a pale tone you can barely see (see page 68). Demonstrate if necessary.
※ Tell the children that they must think carefully about which part of their painting will be the darkest and which the lightest.
※ Ask them to choose a subject. This could be topic-led, or a landscape or portrait will give the children ample opportunities to use a wide range of tones.
※ Explain that they can add more colour to make the tone deeper, but they cannot easily remove colour once it is painted.
※ Ask the children to consider what the background will be. Will it be dark or light, plain or detailed?
※ If they are doing a landscape, point out that the sky will probably be the lightest part of the painting.
※ When they have been painting for a while, point out that they can add detail and texture with a fine brush over colour already painted and dry.

Painting a 'wash'

KEY SKILL

Time
30 min

Resources
Per pair of children:
1 box of watercolour paints
1 water pot
Small palette if required (not really
necessary as the lid will do)

For each child:
1 medium watercolour brush
Cotton wool to wet paper
A paper towel
A4 cartridge paper
A pencil

For the teacher:
Paper to demonstrate

National Curriculum
2a,c, 4a

Year 4 pupil

Introduction

One of the most important skills in watercolour painting is that of painting a wash. Watercolour pictures are often built up in layers, one wash on top of another, and then the picture on top of that. The washes can form the background, or they can be the painting itself, depending on the subject. The paper is heavier than usual painting paper, because it needs to absorb the water, and it is often wetted or dampened before it is painted on. You are going to try laying down a wash on wet, damp and dry paper. The most common use of a wash in a painting is for the sky, and that is what you will do.

Practical activity

❋ Revise how to use the medium if necessary (page 68).

❋ Remind the children not to scrub with the brushes as they will ruin them, and not to leave the brushes standing hair-end down in the water but always to rinse them and lay them down flat on the table.

❋ Tell the children to draw rectangles on their paper as frames for their washes.

❋ Next, demonstrate how to make a wash:
  1. Dip the piece of cotton wool in water, squeeze it out and dampen the rectangle.
  2. Mix up some Prussian blue, get plenty of colour on the brush, then run the side of the brush across the top quarter of the rectangle.
  3. Quickly wash the brush and place the side

of the clean, wet brush at the place where the colour meets the white paper. Then run the side of the brush across the paper and move the colour down the rectangle to about the halfway point.

  4. Wash the brush, place the clean wet brush on the edge of the blue and pull the colour down to the three-quarter point; by now the colour will be a light blue.
  5. Repeat the last step and finish off the lower quarter, covering it with very pale blue paint. This is the same skill as in the previous lesson.
  6. Use a wet brush to spread out and blend any sudden changes of tone.

❋ Emphasize to the children that they will have to move fast. If they dawdle, the paint will dry and they will have a striped sky with bars of colour instead of a graduated wash.

❋ Next, tell them to try making a wash on wet paper, then on dry paper. They could compare the results and experiment. Allow them time to practise making a wash – it is quite an art.

❋ To finish off, they could mix carmine (crimson) to the Prussian blue to make a soft purple and paint the bottom third of one of their skies with this colour.

❋ Next, they could add some Hooker's green to this mixture and paint a bar across the bottom of the page as grass or hills. The colours should blend softly.

❋ Explain to them that this is how they can build up a watercolour picture in layers.

Painting sunsets using a wash

USING SKILL

Time
45 min

Resources
Per pair of children:
1 box of watercolour paints
1 water pot
Small palette if required (not really necessary as the lid will do)

For each child:
1 medium watercolour brush
Cotton wool to wet paper
A paper towel to dab the brush on
A4 heavy cartridge paper or copy of resource sheet 4 on page 119 (or make your own by laying grass across a photocopier)

For the teacher:
1 tin of watercolours to show
Images of sunsets/sunrises/night skies

National Curriculum
2a, 4a, 5a

Andy Brown, Year 4

Note
Photocopier paper is not really good to paint on as it cockles, but if the scenes are quite small and the paint light and delicate, you can just about get away with it.

Introduction
You have practised making a wash, and now you are going to have a go at painting a sunset or night sky like these (show landscape illustrations above). You can see that although the children have used more than one colour, they were still painting a wash.

Practical activity
❋ Revise and practise how to make a wash, and demonstrate if necessary (page 70).
❋ Remind the children not to scrub with the brushes as they will ruin them, and not to leave the brushes standing hair-end down in the water but always to rinse them and lay them down flat on the table.
❋ Children should mix a deep orange (vermilion + gamboge).

❋ Now ask them to dampen the paper with cotton wool and paint a bar of deep orange with the side of their brush across the top quarter of the frame, leaving a circle for the sun.
❋ Next, they should add some gamboge to the orange and a little more water to make a weak and lighter orange. They then dip their brush in this and drag it across over the deep orange at the top of the picture and on down to about the halfway point.
❋ Tell children to quickly wash their brushes, then lay them sideways along the bottom edge of the paler orange and pull the colour down to the bottom of the frame. The picture should start deep orange and fade down to a yellow or pale orange.
❋ Suggest that they experiment with different colour combinations for sunsets, such as deep red down to orange, or dark blue down to pink. They could try an early evening sky by using a deep purple-blue down to pale violet, leaving space for a moon, or a darker, late night sky.

Colour mixing in watercolour (colour sums)

SKILL

| Time |
| 45 min |

Resources
Per pair of children:
1 box of watercolour paints
1 water pot
Small palette if required (not really necessary as the lid will do)

For each child:
1 medium watercolour brush
A paper towel
A4 cartridge paper or copy of resource sheet 5 on page 120
A pencil

For the teacher:
Paper to demonstrate

National Curriculum
2a,c, 4a

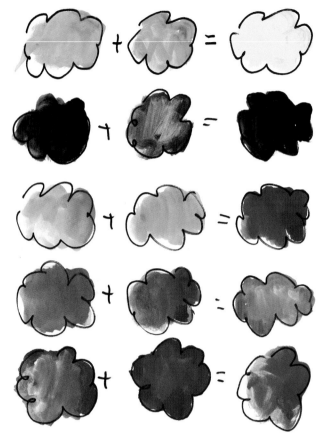

Morgan Johnson, Year 3

Introduction
Today you are going to experiment with mixing the colours in your watercolour box to make new ones. You can make much better paintings if you mix your own colours and use a lot of different colours, than if you just paint with colours straight from the tin.

Practical activity
* Revise how to use the medium if necessary (page 68).
* Remind the children not to scrub with the brushes as they will ruin them, and not to leave the brushes standing hair-end down in the water but always to rinse them and lay them down flat on the table.
* Remind the children to wash their brushes between colours and to change the water frequently.
* Tell them to choose one colour from the tin and paint a dab of that in the first 'cloud' on the resource sheet.

* Next, they should wash their brushes, choose another colour and paint a dab of that in the 'cloud' next to the first.
* Now the children should mix the two colours together and paint the new colour after the equals sign, so that they have a colour sum.
* Suggest they try some more unusual colour combinations, eg:
  * Black + Gamboge =
  * Black + Yellow Ochre =
  * Black + Leaf Green =
  * Black + Burnt Sienna =
  * Burnt Sienna + Prussian Blue =
  * Burnt Sienna + Hooker's Green =
  * Vermilion + Hooker's Green =
* They can paint as many colour combinations as they have time for, and older children might like to devise their own recording system. When dry, the colour mixing results should be stuck into their sketchbooks for future reference.

USING SKILL Colour mixing, and varying the tone in watercolours

Time
1 hour

Link
Music

Resources
Per pair of children:
1 box of watercolour paints
1 water pot
Small palette if required (not really necessary as the lid will do)

For each child:
1 medium watercolour brush
A paper towel
A4 cartridge paper
A pencil and ruler to mark out squares
Fine black pen

For the teacher:
Tape or CD player
Piece of music to play, with clear rhythms and with at least four different instruments

National Curriculum
2a,c, 4a, 5a

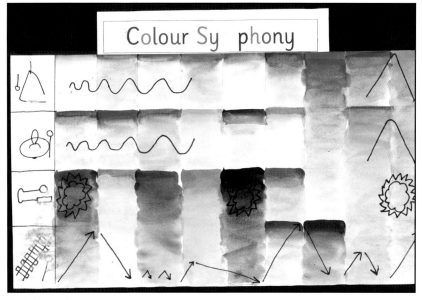

David Riley, Year 4

Introduction
You have tried out mixing lots of new colours and you have learned how to make a colour go lighter and lighter by varying the amount of water on your brush. You are now going to use both of those skills in a painting. Your picture will record the sounds you can hear in colours and marks. Sounds vary in volume, so we will record this by varying the tone of the colour, and you will choose marks and lines to record the speed and rhythms of the music so that other people can guess what was happening in the music.

Practical activity
* First, the children need to mark out their paper into at least six columns and four rows.
* Play the piece of music a few times and ask the children to identify the mood of the piece, the different instruments they can hear and the parts where it is louder/quieter, faster/slower or there are sudden sounds.
* Suggest that they choose four instruments (perhaps by class vote) and draw a little picture of each one down the side of the grid.

* Revise how to use the medium if necessary (page 68).
* Remind the children not to scrub with the brushes as they will ruin them, and not to leave the brushes standing hair-end down in the water but always to rinse them and lay them down flat on the table.
* Remind them also to wash their brushes between colours and to change the water frequently.
* Tell them to try to paint each square in a different colour and to make that colour go from dark at the top of the square to light at the bottom.
* Explain that this is to represent the varying speeds and volumes that the musical notes are played at.
* When all the squares are painted, play the music again and ask them to listen to one of their four instruments.
* Tell them to make marks across the row roughly when the instrument is playing and to try make their marks relate to what the instrument is doing.
* Repeat this for each instrument.
* Play the music again when they have finished and discuss how well their paintings reflect what they can hear.

Painting drawings with watercolours

USING SKILL

Time 45 min Link RE Resources Per pair of children: 1 box of watercolour paints 1 water pot Small palette if required (not really necessary as the lid will do) For each child: 1 medium watercolour brush 1 fine brush A test paper A paper towel to dab the brush on Children's own drawings of buildings (the local church makes a good subject, either photocopied or drawn in permanent ink) National Curriculum 2a, 4a, 5a

Year 4 pupils

Note
Photocopier paper is not really good to paint on as it cockles, but if the scenes are quite small and the paint light and delicate, you can just about get away with it.

Introduction
You have practised mixing colours and you know how to make a wash, so now you are going to have a go at painting your drawings. Try to use light, delicate colours – just a touch of colour will bring your drawings to life. Too much paint, very bright colours or thick paint will tend to deaden them.

Practical activity
* Revise, if necessary, care and use of the media and equipment.
* Remind the children to mix the colours they need and not to be satisfied with the colours in the tin, unless they happen to be the colours they actually want.
* Ask them to consider the time of day, the season and the weather in their scene before they embark on painting. This will affect the colours they choose. Without guidance, children will often just paint skies bright blue, grass bright green and a yellow sun on the corner of the sky. This is easy for them as they don't have to think about it, but it doesn't make for an interesting or atmospheric painting. Ultimately they will see for themselves that it doesn't look good, but at this age they still need gently nudging away from their comfort zones.
* Suggest to the children that they leave some spaces in the sky to be clouds. If the sky is to be grey, they should make the grey using a very pale tone of black with perhaps a tinge of yellow, blue or red, but they should not use white and black to make the grey; it will look heavy and dull.
* Remind them that the sky is usually the lightest part of the picture.
* If the drawings have been photocopied, children could have two or three copies and try out different colours, seasons or weather on each.

Colour mixing with watercolour coloured pencils

SKILL

Time
45 min to 1 hour

Resources
Per group of children:
Box of watercolour pencils

Per pair of children:
1 water pot

For each child:
Sketchbook or A4 cartridge paper
A fine short-handled brush

National Curriculum
4a,b

Tabitha Waldron, Year 3 (watercolour pencils)

Introduction

You can mix and blend colours with coloured pencils, crayons and pastels as well as with paints. Some coloured pencils and crayons are water-soluble, which means that when they are wetted, the colours move and blend. These pencils are watercolour pencils, The coloured 'lead' is made up of solid watercolour pigment and, after you have drawn a mark, you can wet it with a brush dipped in water and the pigment will turn into paint, just as it does when you put a wet brush on a tablet of paint in a paint box.

Practical activity

* First they should try out the different coloured pencils in their sketchbooks.
* Show the children how to make a kind of 'tornado' by using the side of the pencil rather than the point, drawing heavily to begin with and gradually getting lighter to get the full range of tones.

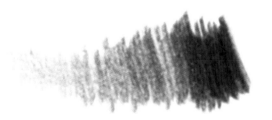

* Then tell them to draw some tornadoes in different colours, and then draw some more in different colours, partly over the top of the first ones. Suggest they try a dark colour over a lighter one, such as brown over yellow, and then a lighter colour over a darker one, to see which blends the best.

* They could try out different colour combinations.
* Next, demonstrate how to dip the brush Into the water, stroke it on the side of the water pot to remove excess water, and then gently wet the colours with the tip of the brush so that they blend.
* Explain that they will need to wash their brushes between colours, just as they would with paint.
* Tell the children to blend some or all of their coloured tornadoes.
* Let them experiment to see just how far a colour will spread and to try to work out how much drawn colour they will need to make a bright or pale shade.
* Now they could try using watercolour pencils in a drawing. It could be anything, topic-led or from their imaginations. However, whatever it is, they need to bear in mind that they are going to blend the colours when they have finished drawing, with a wetted brush.
* Remind the children that a little watercolour pencil goes a long way when it is wetted, and if they want a subtle effect then they need to bear this in mind.

SKILL Wax resist and powdered watercolours (Brusho®)

Time
An afternoon

Link
History/Seaside holidays

Resources
Newspapers for the tables
Oil pastels

For three or four children:
Blue and several other colours of Brusho®, mixed in pots
2–3 medium brushes in each pot
Water pot

For each child:
A3 white cartridge paper
1 fine brush

For the teacher:
Access to pictures of seaside piers
Information about Brusho® on page 11

National Curriculum
2a, 4a, 5a

Ebony Thorne, Year 4 (the end of the pier, in the style of Hundertwasser)

Note

It can be difficult for children to work out which colour is which when the Brusho® is in coloured water pots as the darker colours look very similar, so place a piece of white paper beneath each pot and paint some of the colour from in that pot on the paper. The children can glance at the paper to check the colour inside the pot. If you are really organized (and I have never done this), you could laminate the paper and use it next time.

Introduction

You are going to use the technique of wax resist. The oil in the pastels you will be using will resist the paint and show through. Watercolour paint is excellent for wax resist work as it is thinner and more translucent than powder or ready-mixed paint, so the drawing shows through better.

Practical activity

※ The children should look at pictures of seaside piers and discuss their purposes. Their attention should be drawn to the Victorians' love of decoration: the patterns, lights, cafes, stalls and other embellishments.
※ They should start by drawing a horizontal line, in light blue oil pastel, about a third up from the bottom of the paper. This will be the horizon.

※ Next tell them to draw the sea in blue pastel across the bottom of the paper and add wave patterns.
※ Now, children should draw two black parallel lines about two centimetres apart, horizontally across the middle of the paper.
  • These could be, part the way or all the way across the paper.
  • This is the base of the pier. Tell them to draw in the railings between the two lines.
※ Next, they should look at the pictures of piers again and note the patterns of the iron legs that support them. Then they should draw in their own pier supports. These should run down into the sea.
※ The children can then add whatever attractions they want on the pier: funfairs, shops, lights, cafes, bunting, etc, and then add decoration, such as fancy shaped roofs, curly cast ironwork and some visitors, sea gulls, boats and whatever else they want to create a holiday atmosphere.
※ Now they can paint over their picture in Brusho® in different bright colours, using whatever sized brushes are appropriate. The sea should go right over the legs of the pier, to emphasize the fact that they stand out in the sea.
※ The oil pastels should shine though the Brusho®.

These pictures can be displayed edge-to edge to create one extremely long pier if the children have drawn their own piers right across the paper.

Acrylics

Ruby Petch, Year 4

Introducing acrylic paints

Any paint made from a pigment bound in synthetic resin is commonly known as an acrylic. This term is used whether the resin binder is actually an acrylic or PVA.

Definition that can be read to children

All paints consist of a colour (pigment) and something to bind it together, usually some kind of glue. Acrylic paints are bound together with a kind of plastic. It is quite a recent invention; you could not even buy acrylic paint in Britain until the mid-1960s; it was invented in America.

Acrylic paint is water-based plastic paint that is thick and shiny. It comes in a tube, a tub or a squeezy bottle. You can thin it with water to paint, or you can use it just as it comes. It can even be applied with a palette knife.

Rather like oil paint, acrylic can be painted so thickly that the surface has a texture. Once it is dry, you can paint over the top of it and the new colours won't mix up with the colours underneath. So, you can build up a painting in layers and you can change anything that you want to, but you must wait until it dries. It dries quite quickly, and once it is dry it is waterproof.

WARNING: it will not come out of your clothes, and if it dries on the brushes it will ruin them and they will have to be thrown away. So you must keep acrylic paint off your clothes and wash the brushes out as soon as you have finished with them. You will be pleased to hear, however, that it does come off your skin easily; it washes off when still wet and peels off when it is dry.

A brief history of acrylic paint

The development of acrylic paint came about as the result of pressing social need. In the 1920s, a group of painters in Latin America (mainly Mexico) wanted to paint large murals for public buildings, some of them on exterior walls exposed to the open air. They found that oil paint was unsuitable because it would not last long in such conditions. They experimented with fresco, but this, too, proved impractical.

Year 3 pupil (colour mixing purples and greens)

They needed a paint which would both dry quickly and remain stable in changing climatic conditions. In fact, they needed something which had already existed for some time in the industrial field, but which had not yet been developed as a vehicle for pigments, namely plastic resins. In the 1930s, scientists and artists worked together to develop new paint formulae and many interesting murals and paintings were carried out in New York. Experiments continued in North and South America and painters began to realize that the possibilities went far beyond the needs of exterior murals.

In the 1950s, acrylics appeared on the market in America and they played an important part in the techniques of artists such as Jackson Pollock, Mark Rothko and many others.

Research and development continued, but it was not until the mid-1960s that acrylics were available in Britain. Since then, they have been used by innumerable British artists, including David Hockney and Bridget Riley.

Character of the medium

Acrylic paint is water-soluble but, once the paint is dry, it is waterproof. It dries with a shiny surface and can be wiped.

Acrylic paints can be diluted with water to make a translucent glaze, or used as thickly as in oil painting. They can be applied with a brush or palette knife. This makes them an ideal pre-runner to the introduction of oil paints, or as a similar painting experience for children who may not have the opportunity to use oils.

As soon as the paint is dry, it can be over-painted and, unlike ready-mixed or powder paints, the under-paint colour will not mix with the new colour. Paint can be built up in layers and changes can easily be made if children want to alter anything or rectify mistakes.

Potential pitfalls

Acrylic paint does not come off clothes, and if the brushes are not washed out soon after use they will set rock hard and have to be thrown away. Children will therefore need to wear protective clothing.

The lids need to be closed or replaced immediately after use as the paints dry out quickly. Air should be squeezed out of the tubes before replacing the lids.

Designs for painted cats (see lesson on page 83)

Possible uses

The colours of acrylic paints do not fade and, as the paints are waterproof, they are ideal for exterior murals and sculptures. They can also be used for painting areas in a school where they may get marked or worn, such as in corridors. They are also excellent for painting models and other 3-D objects: twigs, stones, stage props, furniture, etc.

Buying paint

Acrylic paint can be purchased at art stores, but most schools' art suppliers stock it, so this will be the cheaper option. It comes in tubes or tubs, and, in general, a similar range of colours should be used as for watercolours (see page 66). Gold, silver, copper and bronze are also available in acrylics.

It is possible to get children to make their own acrylic paints very cheaply by mixing powder paint or ready-mixed paint and PVA.

Special palettes are not necessary (see environmental tip below).

Brushes

Nylon brushes are excellent for use with acrylic paint as they are tough and are easier to clean. Otherwise, the usual long-handled hog-hair type brushes are fine. It is good to have some flat- (chisel-) ended brushes as well as round ends.

Papers and other surfaces

Acrylics are compatible with a wide variety of surfaces; they can be applied to almost any absorbent support, including canvas, wood, hardboard, card or cartridge paper.

Metal

Acrylics can be used on metal but it might be advisable to lightly sand or rough the surface before painting.

Plastic

Acrylic paint is ideal for painting plastic, much better than ready-mixed or powder paint.

Walls

Crumbling, dirty or powdery surfaces need to be brushed off and made good if necessary, and the area to be painted should be primed with whatever the paint maker recommends (they often have their own recommended primer that goes well with their product).

A useful environmental tip

Lay cling film over the palette, and then put the paint into/onto the palette. At the end of the session, the cling film can be gathered up and thrown away. This will not only reduce the amount of time spent washing up, but reduce the amount of water needed and the amount of chemicals and dyes going down into the drains.

Colour mixing can be done on scrap card which can also be thrown away.

A selection of painted bowls and beakers

Using acrylic paints

KEY SKILL

Time
30 min

Resources
Per pair of children:
1 water pot
1 palette covered in cling film (see note below)

For each child:
2–3 sizes of long-handled brushes
1 thin strip of card
1 plastic knife (for use as palette knife)
A3 cartridge paper
Protective clothing

National Curriculum
2a, 4a

Daniel Huxtable, Year 3

Note: A useful environmental tip
Lay cling film over the palette, and then put the paint into/onto the palette. At the end of the session, the cling film can be gathered up and thrown away. This will not only reduce the amount of time spent washing up, but reduce the amount of water needed and the amount of chemicals and dyes going down into the drains. Colour mixing can be done on scrap card which can also be thrown away.

Introduction
Read the definition of acrylic paint from page 78 or simply explain that acrylic paints are thick water-based plastic paints that can be applied with brushes or a palette knife, and they dry waterproof and slightly shiny. You are going to try out different techniques that you can use with acrylic paint.

Practical activity
* Explain the potential pitfalls to the children (see bottom of page).
* Tell the children to try out the following different effects.
* Use the paint without adding water, and try short brush strokes.
* Paint four patches of thick paint, and in each different patch:
  1. Scratch into it with the corner of a piece of card.
  2. Press the side of the card into it to make a series of lines.
  3. Use the end of the brush to draw spirals and squiggles.

4. When the paint is dry, over-paint with dabs of other colours.
* Tell the children to mix water with the paint to make it much thinner and to try painting a wash in different colours.
* Next, ask them to wash their brushes and use their plastic knives to apply paint thickly – either single colours or several together – so that the paint is raised and textured. They could try scraping the colours together with the side of the knife.
* Suggest to the children that they try applying paint thickly with brushes to make swirls on the surface.
* When the area that was thinly painted is dry, tell the children to over-paint this with patterns with a finer brush, in different colours.
* If there is time, children could experiment with colour mixing.
* Discuss how acrylic paint is different from ready-mixed or powder paint.

Potential pitfalls
* Acrylic paint does not come off clothes, and if the brushes are not washed out soon after use they will set rock hard and have to be thrown away. Children will therefore need to wear protective clothing. The lids need to be closed or replaced immediately after use as the paints dry out quickly. Air should be squeezed out of the tubes before replacing the lids.

Acrylic paints
USING SKILL

Time 2 hours **Resources** Per pair of children: 1 water pot 1 palette covered in cling film (see note on page 81) Acrylic paints including white For each child: 1 medium-sized decorator's brush 2–3 sizes of long-handled brushes 1 plastic knife (for use as palette knife) A3 heavy cartridge paper For the teacher: Access to images of Claude Monet's water lily paintings Information about Monet (page 95) National Curriculum 2a, 4a, 5a

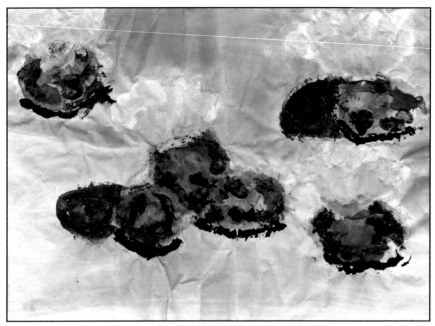

Polly Bray, Year 4

Introduction
You have tried out different techniques with acrylic paints, and now you can try using some of these in a painting.

Practical activity
※ Show images of Monet's water lilies and tell the children that in places he used thick paint. Point out the swirls and brush marks that he made.

※ Tell children the pitfalls of acrylic paint (see Potential pitfalls).

※ Discuss the range of colours Monet used and give the children time to try to mix some of these shades.

※ The children should start by mixing a watery, pale pink or lilac colour. Using the decorator's brush, they should paint a wash, using horizontal brush strokes, to cover the paper. This will be the surface of the water.

※ Next, they should add another wash on top of this in a thin mixture of pale blue paint, but leave some areas of pink showing through.

※ While these washes are drying, the children should mix up some different shades of light and dark green for the lily pads.

※ Then they should paint some lily pads on top of the water, using their palette knives or their brushes. Suggest that they paint the leaves as sideways-elongated ovals to look as if they are lying on top of the water.

※ These will need a little time to dry, so, while they are drying, the children could look again at Monet's paintings of water lilies (of which there are many), note the colours he used and see if they can spot the brush strokes. Explain that these were painted in oil colours – acrylic paint had not been invented in Monet's time.

※ When the leaves are nearly dry, the children should mix up some different whites – pink-whites, yellow-whites, blue-whites, etc – and paint the lily flowers on top of the leaves.

※ Little touches of deeper pink could be added to the petal tips, and further washes of deeper colours could be painted in the water.

Potential pitfalls
Acrylic paint does not come off clothes, and if the brushes are not washed out soon after use they will set rock hard and have to be thrown away. Children will therefore need to wear protective clothing. The lids need to be closed or replaced immediately after use as the paints dry out quickly. Air should be squeezed out of the tubes before replacing the lids.

Painting a 3-D object using acrylic paints (group project)

USING SKILL

Time
2 hours

Link
Multicultural

Resources
Per group of children:
Object to be painted
Selection of brushes in different sizes
1 water pot
1 palette covered in cling film (see note on page 81)
Black, white, brown and yellow paint

For each child:
Permanent pen
B pencil
Sketchbook

For the teacher:
Access to African patterns

National Curriculum
2a,c, 4a,c, 5a,d

Painted cats from three different primary schools

Note
Depending on what is being painted, this could be individual work or a group project. The subject matter will vary, as will the visual resources, but the process will be similar.

Introduction
Acrylic paint is excellent for painting sculpture and other objects. The paint lasts a long time, it can be wiped down if it gets dirty and the colours stay bright. You are going to use acrylic paint to paint (whatever it is that is going to be painted). (In this example it was a wooden cat that had been purchased in advance as part of a fundraising project. The painted cats were auctioned and the money sent to Africa for various art projects in schools.)

Practical activity
* Show images of African patterns and tell the children to look at the colours, shapes and lines that have been used.
* Ask them to try copying a few patterns in their sketchbooks and then to create some of their own.
* The group should then discuss which patterns it likes the best and choose one from each group member. The group could then decide where on the cat the patterns will

go. They could design a composite cat which includes all their ideas.
* Next, the children take it in turns to use the permanent pens to draw their patterns onto the cat.
* Remind the children of the pitfalls of acrylic paint (see Potential pitfalls).
* Discuss the range of colours to be used and give children time to try to mix some different browns by adding yellow or black or white to the existing brown.

Possible finishing touches
* A necklace could be made for the cat using clay beads, which the children could paint when the clay has dried.
* Wire or string could be wound around the cat's neck, and other objects attached.
* The patterns could be redefined with black permanent pen outlines.
* Dots and stripes can be over-painted when the first coat is dry to add to the patterns.

Potential pitfalls
* Acrylic paint does not come off clothes, and if the brushes are not washed out soon after use they will set rock hard and have to be thrown away. Children will therefore need to wear protective clothing. The lids need to be closed or replaced immediately after use as the paints dry out quickly. Air should be squeezed out of the tubes before replacing the lids.

History of painting

Daniel Huxtable, Year 3

A few key pointers in the history of painting

Note: this is suitable for reading to the children.

Cave paintings (at least 20,000 years ago)

The earliest paintings have been found in caves all over the world. Prehistoric people lived at the entrances to these caves and the paintings have been found deep inside them. There are many pictures of the animals the people hunted, such as bison, horses, stags and even woolly rhinoceroses. From these paintings we know about extinct animals, such as the mammoth. There are various theories about why they were painted, but some historians think they were part of the hunting ritual and would bring good luck in a hunt. Other experts think that the caves where the paintings are found might have been places of worship.

Some famous caves in France were discovered by accident. Some boys were out for a walk with their dog, and the dog disappeared down a hole in the hillside. One of the boys went to search for him. The ground beneath the boy's feet gave way and he tumbled into a cave, followed by his friends. They lit matches to see where they were, and were amazed to find hundreds of animals painted on the walls.

Tho prehistoric artists used soil and rocks to make red-brown, black, yellow ochre and white colours. They mixed them with clay, crushed them and added water or animal fats to make them liquid. The paints were kept in hollowed-out bones, which were plugged at one end. The artists painted with their fingers or used brushes made of twigs with chewed ends. Pads of fur and moss were also used, and they worked by the light of animal fat lamps.

Egyptian painting (approximately 3,000 years ago)

Survival was the chief preoccupation for prehistoric people, but the people of ancient Egypt had the wealth and leisure to create objects which were ornamental and not just functional. However, survival still played its part, as the Egyptians believed in life after death. Pictures were painted on the walls of the tombs of their kings, and many beautiful objects were placed in the tombs to help the buried kings and queens in their next lives.

The Egyptian artists followed strict rules about the way figures were represented: the head was in profile, the shoulders and eyes were viewed from the front and the legs and feet were again viewed from the side, with their feet invariably being depicted facing the same way. Egyptians believed that this showed the human figure to its best advantage.

The Egyptian artists were specially trained to paint spells on coffins and scenes on the walls of tombs of kings and other important people. People believed the spells would protect the dead, and that the scenes would work by magic to give them everything they needed for living in the next world.

The artists ground their own colour from minerals and used charcoal (burnt wood) for black and ochre for red.

The Egyptians invented six colours to paint with (see page 87); before that artists had only been able to use black, white and earth colours.

Jasmine Hammot, Year 0

European illuminated manuscripts (approximately 1,200 years ago)

The pages of medieval manuscripts were often brilliantly decorated with gold leaf and bright colours. These were done by hand by monks in monasteries. The illustrated books took years to produce. Bibles and prayer books were illustrated with tiny scenes, which were sometimes painted below the writing and sometimes inside the capital letter of the first line of a new paragraph or chapter. The text was often surrounded by beautifully painted and richly patterned borders.

The paints they used were made by the monks or their assistants. They used egg tempera, which is a paint made by mixing egg yolk with ground powdered colours (pigments). Some of the pigments were crushed semi-precious stones such as lapis lazuli, which is a beautiful blue. Where lapis lazuli has been used, the blue is as bright today as it was when it was painted hundreds of years ago. The blue is a bit like the brilliant blue or ultramarine that we use today, and it was as valuable as gold. They also used gold itself, which had been made as thin as tissue paper (this is called 'gold leaf'), to decorate their books.

Maya Barker, Year 3

European art (until about 200 years ago)

The subject matter of most paintings in Europe until about 200 hundred years ago was either religious or portraits of wealthy and important people. Kings, queens, popes, other rulers and churches or cathedrals might commission paintings of religious scenes or portraits of themselves, their families and their property. There were also specific subjects for paintings, such as still life and landscapes, and there were rules about what should be included in the painting and where. The person who asked for and paid for the painting would say what they wanted to be in it – it wasn't up to the artist. Some kings and queens loved art more than others and would have several artists working for them creating beautiful things.
Artists often worked in studios with other artists, and their apprentices mixed paints and learned to paint specific things like folds in clothing, hands or backgrounds.

Artists needed to find someone rich or important who would sponsor them and commission them to do paintings, or a studio who would take them on. They might have to pay for the privilege or find someone who would pay for their apprenticeship for them.

Colours

It is interesting to remember that in the past, an artist's palette was restricted by availability; the colours that we paint with today were not always available, and some were very expensive. Many paints have unusual names. They are often named after the plant, rock, earth, animal or place they come from.

Children might like to hear about these:
* Dragon's blood was the name of a pigment made from a fruit – not, as people thought, made from real dragon's blood.
* Indian yellow was a yellow pigment from India that was made by heating the urine of cows fed on mango leaves.
* Lampblack comes from soot which is made by burning oil or fat.
* Raw sienna is an earth colour made from a natural clay containing iron; burnt sienna is raw sienna that has been roasted.
* Tyrian purple was made from crushed shellfish. This was such an expensive pigment it was used to dye the robes of the emperors in ancient Rome, and purple is still considered to be a royal colour today.

A timeline of colours

Some colours are very old and some relatively modern.

20,000 BC	Burnt wood (black)
	Chalk (white)
	Ochre (yellow-brown made from earth)
	Umber (brown made from earth)
	Other earth colours, eg red-brown
1000–2000 BC	Blue frit (known also as Egyptian Blue)
	Malachite (green made from copper)
	Realgar orange (contains arsenic)
	Cinnabar red (contains mercury)
	White lead (white)
	Lemon yellow
100 BC	Indigo (dark blue made from a plant)
	Tyrian purple (made from a whelk)
	Verdigris (green)
12–1300 AD	Lead-tin yellow
	Madder (ruby red made from a plant)
	Vermilion (light red made from the mineral cinnabar)
	Ultramarine (blue made from lapis lazuli)
1700	Prussian blue (dark blue)
1750	Naples yellow (made with lead)
1800	Cobalt blue
1817	Cadmium yellow
1820	Chrome yellow
1828	Ultramarine (blue) – a synthetic version
1830s	Zinc white
1856	Perkins mauve
1861	Cobalt yellow
1910	Cadmium red
1916	Titanium white
1918	Cadmium orange

After this, many more colours were manufactured using chemicals, and there is now a huge range of colours available to artists.

Tabitha Waldron, Year 3

SKILL Cave paintings, part 1: making your own paint, charcoal and brushes

Time
1 hour

Links: History/Design and Technology

Resources
Newspapers to cover tables
Earth, sieved to remove stones and wildlife (you could use garden-centre soil)
Collection of dry twigs to burn
Lighter/matches
Ice cream tubs to collect and mix earth
Large lump of white chalk (or sticks of chalk)
1 flat stone and 1 heavy stone for grinding chalk
Vegetable oil
Water
Green twigs, feathers, moss, string, grasses, etc

Per group of 4–5 children:
2 water pots to hold paints

For each child:
Protective clothing

For the teacher:
Access to images of cave paintings
Nerves of steel
Second adult to assist

National Curriculum
2a,c, 3a, 4a,c, 5a,d

Note
Be aware of health and safety issues when making the twig bonfire and when children are handling earth; make a risk assessment and follow school guidelines.

Introduction
Read the information on cave paintings to children on page 85 and show images of cave paintings.

Practical activity
* Tell the children that they are going to try making their own paints and their own brushes, just as the cave people did, and that later they will be painting with them.

* If possible, go out into the school garden or grounds with the children and collect earth and dead dry twigs.
* Also collect green twigs, moss, grasses, feathers and anything else that could conceivably be used or might have been used by cave people to make brushes.

Making charcoal
* One adult, and possibly a small group of children, should remain and build a small bonfire of the twigs. This should be left to burn itself out. If the twigs are thin, they will burn up quite quickly.
* The cooled burnt twigs can be collected later when the paint and brushes have been made.

Making brushes
* Explain to the children that they could make brushes by tying leaves, grasses, moss or thin twigs to a twig handle (they could cheat here and use string to tie the bits and bobs on).
* The other way they can make brushes is to take a green twig and bash the ends of the twig between two stones until it frays out a little. Fibres can then be separated further with their fingers.

Making paint
* White paint:
  * The chalk should be ground to a powder by crushing it between two stones. Children could also try breaking the chalk sticks into small pieces and then crushing them inside a paper towel.
  * Next, the powder should be collected into one pot; just a little vegetable oil and some water added will make a thin paste. Quite a bit will be needed for the whole class.
* Brown paint:
  * The earth should gradually be mixed with water and vegetable oil until it reaches a paint-like consistency. Powdered chalk or charcoal could be added to make the brown lighter or darker.
  * The paints and charcoal can now be distributed among the children so they can now do their cave paintings.

Stone age palette, earth paint, paint made with ground chalk, home-made brushes, ground red stone and pounding stone.

Potential pitfalls

❋ Some of the home-made brushes will undoubtedly fall apart during the painting session or will not work as well as they might, especially if children have used too large a twig or have not tightly secured the hairy part of the brush to the handle. These children will need to continue with school brushes.

❋ The children may get carried away when they are mixing up the earth paint!

Luke Bray, Year 3

SKILL Cave paintings, part 2 (can be done with or without making your own paints, brushes and charcoal)

Time
1 hour

Resources
Newspaper to cover tables

Per group of 4–5 children:
Home-made paints, etc
2 water pots to hold paints
A pile of burnt twigs
Home-made brushes
4–5 spare school brushes, in case
Resources if not making paints, etc:
Newspapers for tables
Sticks of white chalk
Charcoal
Brown chalky pastels or
Brown paint, paintbrush and water
in pots

For all children:
Protective clothing
Sketchbook and pencil
A3 brown or stone-coloured paper

For the teacher:
Access to images of cave paintings
and horses, deer, bison, and wild
boar.

National Curriculum
2a,c, 3a, 4a,c, 5a,d

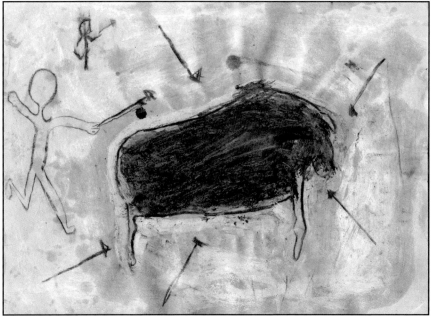

Isabelle Kennedy-Brown, Year 3

Note

This lesson works very well if the children make their own paints, but it also can be done using school charcoal, brushes, chalk, brown pastels or paint. It does have more impact when the children make their own materials, but this can be very messy and time-consuming. Ironically, the end results often look better when they have used shop-bought products. The home-made variety can look like a pig's breakfast, but the children love doing it.

Introduction

Read the information on cave paintings to children on page 85. Tell the children that they are going to make some paintings similar to those found in the caves.

Practical activity

 ❋ Look at the images of cave paintings and discuss the colours and the content.

Encourage the children to speculate about how and why the paintings were made and what living conditions might have been like.
 ❋ Children should now look at images of cows, deer, bison, etc and sketch some in their sketchbooks. (The children who did the work illustrated here and on pages 84 and 89 went to draw cows that were grazing in a field across from the playground, but the wretched animals went and lay down, so you can't win!)
 ❋ Next, the children should draw on their brown paper, using their charcoal, one large (appropriate, eg not a guinea pig!) animal of their choice in the middle of the page, and possibly some arrows and hunters.
 ❋ Tell the children to colour the background white, using either their home-made paint and brushes or a piece of chalk. This will make the animal stand out as it is on brown paper.
 ❋ Now they should colour the animal brown with either home-made brown paint, school paint or brown pastels. If they are using their own brushes, they won't be able to wash them, so tell them to just dip the brush in the earth paint; it will come out patchy, which will look quite authentic.
 ❋ Details such as cracks on the wall, fur or markings on the animals, etc can be added last.

ACTIVITY # Egyptian painting

Time
2 hours
Link
History
Resources
Newspaper to cover tables
Per pair of children:
Powder paint or ready-mixed:
• ultramarine (brilliant blue), white, black, vermilion, lemon yellow
• gold ready-mixed paint
1 water pot
1 palette
For each child:
1 fine long-handled brush
1 fine watercolour brush
A4 cartridge paper
Sketchbooks or paper
Test paper
For the teacher:
Access to images of Egyptian tomb paintings
National Curriculum
1c, 4a,b,c, 5a,d

Will Ayres, Year 4

Introduction

Today you are going to do some paintings in the style and colours of the ancient Egyptians. They used particular colours because only some colours had been invented in paint form at that time. They created six new colours and a new kind of white, and you will also be using gold as gold is a colour that they used a lot of in their jewellery, masks and sculptures.

Practical activity

✳ Read children the section on Egyptian painting on page 85 and the BC section of the colour timeline on page 87.

✳ Show some images of tomb paintings and discuss the way the human figure is portrayed.

✳ Ask children to try to stand in the same way the figures stand, with the head facing to the side, shoulders to the front and feet both facing the same way. They will find it very hard to balance and will realize how unnatural tho pose io.

✳ Tell the children they are going to try to draw a put-together figure – the head of one person, the shoulders of another and so on.

✳ Ask one child to pose for the profile of the head and face.

✳ Tell the children to draw one eye as seen from the front.

✳ Next ask another child to pose, facing the class, for the shoulders and body.

✳ The last model should stand sideways, with one leg in front of the other and feet facing the same way.

✳ Now tell them to draw a similar figure on their paper and add ancient Egyptian clothes and a collar and headdress, or draw an animal's head.

✳ They should now paint the drawing using only the colours available to the Egyptian artists:
  ○ Ultramarine (to be blue frit)
  ○ White
  ○ Vermilion (to be cinnabar)
  ○ Orange
  ○ Lemon yellow
  ○ A yellow-brown (ochre)
  ○ Bright green (malachite)
  ○ Brown (umber)
  ○ Black

✳ Lastly they could paint the background gold, just for effect.

SKILL

Medieval art: illuminated letters

Time
2 hours

Link
RE
History

Resources
Newspaper to cover tables

Per pair of children:
Powder paint or ready-mixed:
• crimson + vermilion red
• cyan + brilliant blue
• brilliant + lemon yellow
(or a tin of watercolours)
Gold ready-mixed paint
1 water pot
1 palette

For each child:
Watercolour brushes, fine and
medium sizes
A4 cartridge paper
Sketchbooks or paper
Test paper
1 fine-line black pen

For the teacher:
Access to images of illuminated
manuscripts

National Curriculum
1c, 4a,b,c, 5a,d

Prince Sexon, Year 4

Introduction
Today you are going to design and paint your own
illuminated letters. (Read the section on European illuminated
manuscripts on page 86.)

Practical activity
❋ Show the children the images of the
illuminated lettering and explain that the
scene depicted inside or around the letter
often related to the content of the paragraph.
❋ Ask them to choose the first letter of one of
their names and ask them to design a letter
in their sketchbooks and decorate the letter
itself. If they want to, they can place some
images about themselves in the background,
or take ideas from illuminated letters that they
have been shown, or they could simply use
patterns and shapes they like.
❋ Remind them that the monks would have

taken weeks, maybe months, over one tiny
painting, and ask them to take time and
trouble with their designs.
❋ When they have completed the design, it
could be photocopied to save the children
doing it again, or they could copy it onto
white paper.
❋ Next, tell them to paint it in using bright,
jewel-like colours.
❋ Explain to the children that the monks would
have considered their art to be 'to the glory
of their God' and so would want to do their
very best work as part of their worship.
❋ Remind them that the blue and gold were
incredibly expensive and that the monks
would have used them very carefully and
sparingly.
❋ When the painting is dry, children could go
over the outlines with a black fine-line pen.

Using works of art

Steve Latham, Year 3 (in the style of Georgia O'Keeffe)

Artists and art movements

Children gain confidence through the ability to handle and control a substance as complex as paint, and by being able to express and communicate ideas through painting. Learning about the way artists, past and present, have used paint can extend the range of possibilities for children in their knowledge and in their thinking.

Studying the works of an artist, whether famous or relatively unknown, is often an excellent way of trying out the techniques favoured by various art movements.

It is essential to have access to a good supply of materials, such as prints of paintings by your chosen artists. These do not have to be expensive items – they can be old calendars, cut up and laminated, birthday or Christmas cards, or even old art books which are too tatty to use in the library, cut up and laminated.

Shops that sell remaindered books are an excellent source of art books, but be careful to go through them and make sure there are no unsuitable images. I do not mean nudes, as these are part of classical art history and children need to get used to seeing these without

sniggering, but there can be really unsuitable images, including those that are violent, disturbing or erotic. For example, check before you consider using any books on Klimt, because of his erotic drawings.

If you have an interactive whiteboard in the class or art room, a brilliant way to share larger images of works of art with children is to use the Internet. Open up Google and click on 'Images', then type in either an artist or the subject you want, and then click 'search' again. You will be presented with a number of thumbnail images and, if you click again on these, you will get a larger image. Some will have 'see full size image' written below, and you can click on this to bring the picture up full size.

The National Gallery's website has a wonderful zoom facility whereby you can zoom in on any area of the picture and see it in detail. Try it with Fra Filippo Lippi's Annunciation and you can even see the tiny slit in the skirts of the stomach area where the spirit of God is about to enter. Or, try Canaletto's 'Stonemason's yard', where you can zoom in and show the children where the fallen toddler is weeing himself in surprise. They will like that!

Year 4 pupil (in the style of Hundertwasser)

Particularly useful artists to use with children

Paul Klee (Swiss, 1879–1940)
Used in Basic skills (page 31)

Paul Klee is a wonderful artist to use with children as his work has a childlike quality. He was fascinated with children's artwork and children relate well to this quality, which makes his work accessible to them and non-threatening.

Klee worked on colour mixing in a progressive series of works as part of his teaching at the Bauhaus design school in West Germany. Many of his experiments were carried out in the form of beautiful small watercolours, painted in many overlapping layers of transparent colour, mostly based on just two colours. Many of his paintings show a range of colours juxtaposed, and these are excellent for children to look at when learning about colour mixing or colour relationships.

Henri Rousseau (French, 1844–1910)
Rousseau is particularly useful to use if children have been studying wild animals, green colour mixing or jungles. Children might like to know that he never went to the jungle or ever saw any wild animals or jungle plants, except in the zoological gardens in Paris. His style is slightly naive, which makes it easy for children to relate to.

Georges Seurat (French, 1859–1891)
Seurat's experimentation with colour – and in particular his idea that the colours could be painted separately in small dots or dashes and the eye of the viewer would do the colour mixing – makes him an interesting artist to work with when children are studying either the art movement to which he belonged ('Pointillism') or colour mixing and colour theory.

Georgia O'Keeffe (American, 1887–1986)
Used in Using works of art (page 101)

Georgia O'Keeffe's large dramatic paintings of flowers, often painted in single colours or just two colours, are ideal for children to look at when they are painting for any reason in a restricted palette (perhaps because they are investigating a range of one colour or are experimenting with simple colour mixing). Her paintings have tremendous mood and impact.

Claude Monet (French, 1840–1926)
Used in Acrylic paints (page 82)

Monet is an inspirational artist to tell children about. He would paint the same scene over and over again to capture it in different lights, times of day, weather conditions and seasons. Children can be shown his series of paintings of haystacks, water lilies or cathedrals, or of the famous gardens at Giverny – all paintings of the same scenes but in different colours. They can look at his works if they are studying subtle differences in colours, and also if they are concentrating on brush strokes. It is easy for them to see these in many of his paintings.

Vincent Van Gogh (Dutch, 1853–1890)
Used in Other techniques and media (page 108)

Van Gogh's vigorous brush marks are clear for children to see. They can see the passion and mood of his paintings and discuss his vivid use of colour. Children are often interested to hear that Van Gogh was a late starter who didn't begin drawing until he was 26 and wasn't very good to start with. They might also like to hear about his powerful emotions, to know that he tried to cut off his own ear, that he loved the colour yellow and that Don McLean's song 'Vincent' ('Starry starry night … ') was written about him. Films have also been made of his life story.

Francis Huntingford, Year 3 (in the style of Georgia O'Keeffe)

Franz Marc (German, 1880–1916)

Marc's use of strong bold colours, often combined with black, are dramatic and appealing to children – particularly his paintings of animals.

Marc Chagall (Russian, 1887–1985)

Chagall painted many dream-like paintings which feature stories, family scenes such as weddings and parties, and other aspects of his life in Russia. The slightly childlike folk quality of many of his pictures appeals to children and is a good source for paintings on a dream theme.

Gustav Klimt (Austrian, 1862–1918)

Klimt's work is a glorious mixture of colours, patterns and textures. He uses gold, golden yellows and brilliant jewel-like colours in his works, and the subject matter is often heavy with symbolism. While a lot of his works are semi-erotic (check for this before you use any books on his work), there are a number of works that are inspirational for children to work from, eg 'The tree of life', 'Portrait of Adele Bloche-Bauer 1' and his 'Apple tree', 'Poppy field' and 'Sunflower'.

Wassily Kandinsky (Russian, 1866–1944)

Used in Colour theory (page 62)

Kandinsky's use of brilliant colours and often non-figurative compositions make him an excellent artist to use with even very young children, especially when they are just concentrating on working in colour. His work is distinctive and children can easily recognize it. He worked in a group of artists in a movement called 'The Blue Rider', which included Paul Klee, Franz Marc and August Macke, all of whom are wonderful artists to use with children. He was possibly the first 'abstract' artist.

Robert Delauney (French, 1885–1941)

Delauney was a pioneer of abstract art who painted some compositions which were of pure colour in concentric circles. These are a good starting-point for children when mixing and painting colours as the composition is not daunting, and you can explain to the children that he was experimenting with different colour combinations.

Friedrich Hundertwasser (Austrian, 1928–2000)

Used in Using works of art (page 102)

Hundertwasser's work is extraordinary; he was an architect as well as a painter. It is very difficult to describe his work, as his paintings are full of brilliant colours and lines and often include houses in the compositions. He, rather like the Catalan architect Gaudi, loved to soften

Emily Sweet, Year 3 (in the style of Hundertwasser)

the contours of buildings with curved edges and organic forms. Children respond well to his colourful and unusual paintings and they are a good vehicle for wax resist pictures because of his use of line and colour.

Pablo Picasso (Spanish, 1881–1973)

Picasso is an inspirational artist to use with children because of the enormous range of his work, which includes not only painting but also ceramics, sculpture, collage and graphics. They need to understand that he could draw superbly by the age of 15 and spent the rest of his life experimenting and pushing artistic boundaries. One of the aspects of Picasso that is so inspiring is the sheer force of his creativity and the fact that he was still trying new styles and ideas in his 90s.

Joseph Turner (British, 1775–1851)

Turner is probably one of Britain's best-known painters, along with Constable. Turner was a master at painting light and the energy of the elements. Children might like to hear that the inspiration for a painting called 'Snow storm' arose when he was tied to the mast of a boat for four hours during a terrible storm, and he later painted this picture based on his experience. He is an excellent artist for children to study when they are using watercolours and are trying to get a feeling of lightness and brightness, particularly in skies.

Amadeo Modigliani (Italian 1884–1920)

Modigliani is probably the archetypal 'bohemian' artist who loved, lived and drank well but not wisely. He was passionate, romantic, good-looking and died young. He was also a brilliant artist. His work is very distinctive as his portraits tend to have elongated faces and necks. He was much influenced by African sculptures and masks. Children might like to hear that in a fit of passion and depression, he threw many of his sculptures in the river Seine in Paris.

Piet Mondrian (Dutch 1872–1944)

A lot (but not all) of Mondrian's works are easily recognizable as he uses similar pictorial elements in them: the straight line, the horizontal line, the primary colours, red, yellow and blue and the non-colours black, grey and white. For this reason, he is excellent to use as a starting-point for work on learning the primary colours. Simple Mondrian-like paintings are easily achievable by even quite young children. This work can be combined with maths, in the study of right angles, rectangles and squares. He was part of an art group known as 'De Stijl'.

Jackson Pollock (American 1912–1956)

Jackson Pollock was a pioneer of an art movement called 'Action painting'; he would throw, spray, trickle or splatter the paint on top of the surface of the canvas layer upon layer, building up a highly patterned and textured surface. He would even ride a bike over it. The action involved in the making of the painting was as important as the look of the final artwork. Children will enjoy using some of his techniques: different colours of paint can be dribbled from squeezy bottles onto the paper and toy cars can be run through the paint. This works as well with very young children as it does with older ones.

Some art movements of the 19th and 20th century

Here are some art movements that you might want to refer to at some point with your pupils. Many of them are mentioned at some point in this book.

Fauves (based in Paris in the 1900s)

Known as the 'wild beasts', they used brilliant colour, often not as seen in nature. Their subject matter was really colour itself. Artists include André Derain, Henri Matisse and Maurice Vlaminck

Pre-Raphaelites (mainly French and British, 1848 onwards)

They painted very realistically, often depicting romantic scenes from medieval England, from Shakespeare, legends and poems. Children may enjoy hearing the stories behind the paintings: the Arthurian legends or 'The Lady of Shalott'. The Pre-Raphaelites are much scorned by art snobs.

Impressionists (Europe, 1860s onwards)

The Impressionists, as the name suggests, were interested in capturing an impression – a fleeting moment of light and atmosphere. They were revolutionary at the time in showing loose brush marks and not tight realism, and their paintings met with violent negative responses from the established art world. The most famous artists involved in the movement were Monet, Renoir, Manet, Sisley, Degas and Cézanne.

Post-Impressionists (Dutch and French,1880s)

Some artists turned away from the ideas of the Impressionists and went their own way. The most famous of these were Paul Gauguin and Vincent Van Gogh, two artists who had a turbulent friendship and greatly influenced each other's work.

Cubism (Europe, end of 19th century)

This movement abandoned traditional methods, perspective and vision, portraying a subject from several viewpoints, searching for and emphasizing its geometric forms. Cézanne was the first cubist and he inspired others such as Picasso and Braque.

Abstract painting (Europe, end of 19th century onwards)

This is generally considered to be non-representational art, ie it does not attempt to represent nature or any recognizable subject matter. Kandinsky was the artist who made the first step towards complete abstraction.

Another sub-group of artists who could also be called abstract artists were known as 'De Stijl', a movement that was formed in Holland in 1917. Their paintings contained mainly horizontal and vertical lines, and the most famous exponent was Mondrian.

Surrealism (Europe, 1923 onwards)

This was an art movement which stressed the importance of the irrational and the subconscious. Surrealist paintings are often quite strange and can be disturbing to children. The most famous exponent is the Spanish artist Salvador Dali.

Dada (Switzerland 1914)

The Dadaists were a group of artists who wanted to produce art that shocked people, just as the First World War, which was then starting,

Thomas Parkhouse, Year 4 (in the style of Picasso)

was shocking. The name Dada was chosen at random, but it is in fact a French word for a child's rocking horse. The Dada artists were very anti-art, and had their own ideas of art that were not the same as those of the rest of society. Marcel Duchamp was an artist working in this movement. He liked to take ready-made objects and exhibit them as art in galleries. His most famous work in this genre, the children might like to hear, was a urinal.

Action painting (USA, 1950s)

These paintings were sometimes painted using the hands directly on the canvas, or by throwing or dribbling the paint onto the canvas. The artwork was as much about the actual movement and the physical involvement of the artist as it was about the way the painting looked. Children generally thoroughly enjoy having a go at this!

Pop art (USA, 1960s)

In the 1960s, the music of the Beatles was heard throughout the world. Art could also become 'pop' like music. Pop artists welcomed the images we see today, such as cans of Coke, advertisements and comic books. The artists working in this movement used the mass production of their age to produce their work, which often includes repeated images. These reflect posters and the rows of products that could be found on supermarket shelves (supermarkets themselves were new in the 1960s). Iconic images from films and television were often taken and altered. Andy Warhol was one of the artists working in this style.

'Op' art (Britain, 1960s)

Op art is short for 'optical art'. The artists working in this movement were interested in deceiving the eye of the viewer in different ways, creating optical illusions. Work was often in black and white and very sharp and well defined. The British artist Bridget Riley was a major exponent of op art, but she also worked in dazzling colours that contrasted and created strong after-images in complementary colours. Her research was highly mathematical and exact, and the illusions she created were not there by chance.

Naïve and Primitive artists

This is not an art movement but a style or type of art. It is often used to describe the work of artists who have received no formal training in art, who have come to painting relatively late in life, or who use aspects of folk art extensively or have a childlike quality. Rousseau and Lowry could be described as having Naïve qualities.

Questioning that will enhance children's responses to and understanding of works of art

What do children gain from looking at art?

Children gain two huge advantages from looking at art. The first is that they learn about their heritage as artists – whether that heritage is national or worldwide. For this, they need to see as wide a variety of paintings as possible, so that their working definitions are flexible and generous.

The second gain is to children's own artwork and working methods. Children who have examined other art forms will work with greater technique (provided they have been led to consider how the work was done) and a greater openness about what their painting materials can do. Hopefully, they will also have been inspired by the passion and interest communicated by the teacher. With careful choice of artworks and skilful questioning, children can be led, open-eyed and open-hearted, into the world of the visual arts.

How to access works of art

If the teacher has access to an interactive whiteboard, and most classrooms do have them now, it is relatively easy to download large-scale images of works of art so that children may look at the image at the same time and share their responses. The easiest way is to use the Google search engine (www.google.co.uk) and click on 'Images'. In the search box, enter the image or artist you want and this will bring up a selection of images to choose from.

If an interactive whiteboard is not an option (perhaps work is taking place in an art room where there is no board, or a board is not available for whatever reason), then the school will need to build up a collection of reproductions of works of art, from postcard-sized reproductions to large posters. If the school has contact with a local artist who is able to lend or come and show some of their work, then this opportunity should be exploited. To hear an artist talk about their work is a powerful experience, as is hearing background information about art from an art expert.

In the absence of artists or art experts, however, there are many different ways to encourage children to respond to a work of art, to draw them in and to involve them. The teacher can talk about the painting and the children can also talk about it.

What to say and what to ask

Questions the teacher might ask break down into four areas:

* Description: what do you see?
* Analysis: how are things put together?
* Interpretation: what is the artist trying to say?
* Judgement: what do you think of it?

It is probably best to ask children what they see, know and think before we tell them what we see, know and think, although it is tempting to talk first when we are sharing a picture we know and to which we have a strong response ourselves. Between the whole class, they may spot more than we think they will. If we have some information and questions ready, we can fill in the gaps and extend their understanding.

Possible questions might include:

Opening questions

* What do you see?
* Do you like the painting?
* Why?
* What is going on in the picture?
* Do you think there is a story behind it?
* What time of year, day and season do you think it is?
* Do you think it was painted long ago, a while ago, or quite recently?
* Is it realistic (lifelike)?

Colour

* Is the painting bright and colourful?
* Are the colours mostly pale/all in one colour/dark?
* Is there one colour that stands out (a dominant colour)?
* Why is this?
* Does that colour help the mood?
* Has the artist used hot/cold/complementary/harmonious/earth colours?
* How does this help to convey the feeling?
* What (kinds of) colours have been used?

* Are the colours 'real life colours'?
* Why is the sky that colour?
* Is it painted that colour to help create an atmosphere?

Portraits

* Do you know, or have you heard of, the person in the painting?
* Do you think they would have liked it?
* How many people are in the picture?
* What do you think this or that person is thinking/feeling?
* What might they say if they could speak to you?
* Can you see any groups of people within the picture?
* What are they doing?
* Why do you think the artist has put them in?
* How would you describe the clothes they are wearing?
* Which one would you like/not like to be?

General

* Where do you think the light is coming from?
* What might have happened before/after this moment?
* Can you see the artist's brush strokes?
* How do you think the artist has done that?
* Why do you think they chose this subject?
* What medium has the artist used (watercolour, oil paint, etc)?
* Why do you think they chose to use (whatever medium it is)?
* What shapes can you find?
* Would you buy this picture?
* Is there anything in the painting that might be symbolic?
* Why do you think this picture was painted?
* How has the (specific things such as clouds, hair, hills, etc) been painted?
* How does this picture make you feel?
* What do you think of it?
* If you had painted it, is there anything you would have changed?
* What do you think the artist was feeling when they painted this?
* How has the artist made things look far away/close to?
* How did the artist create the mood of the painting?

* Do you think they enjoyed painting it?
* Why do you think that?
* Does the painting remind you of the work of another artist?
* Have you seen the painting before? If so, where?
* Is it a successful painting? Why do you think that? Who thinks something different?
* Where was the painting made to be seen – a private house, a church, a gallery, or some other public place?

Once the first few questions start and children make different responses, it is quite easy to extend this by asking children if they agree or disagree with what someone else has said.

It is important, when the children are discussing their own responses to a work of art, that they understand that they are entitled to have an opinion that is different from those of others. They should know that the artist may well have wanted people to look at their work and have very different responses. Children must feel free to make comment without fear of censure from other children.

Year 4 pupil (in the style of Paul Klee)

Using the work of Georgia O'Keeffe

Time
1–2 hours

Resources
Newspaper to cover tables
Purple flowers, eg iris, pansies, or
pictures of them

Per pair of children:
Powder paint or ready-mixed colours:
- crimson and vermilion red
- cyan and brilliant blue
- lemon and brilliant yellow
Oil pastels for detail
1 water pot and 1 palette

For each child:
1 medium long-handled brush
Cartridge paper
Test paper

For the teacher:
A3 piece of paper to demonstrate the
colours
Masking tape
Access to the work of Georgia O'Keeffe
Information about O'Keeffe (page 95).

National Curriculum
2a, 4a, 5a

Damian Hopkins, Year 3

Note
This work can be done with poppies and makes a
lovely Remembrance Day display.

Introduction
*The artist Georgia O'Keeffe painted paintings of flowers and
plants in a very dramatic way. She would often use just one or
two colours and she would make the flower heads fill the page.
You are going to paint some flowers in a similar way to her.*

Practical activity
※ Show the children some paintings by the artist.
※ Ask the children which two primary colours
 are mixed together to make purple.
※ Explain that brilliant blue and crimson make
 the best purples and cyan and vermilion
 make a rather browny-purple.
※ Ask them to experiment mixing up different
 purples (or whatever colours are appropriate),
 and to paint little dabs of these colours
 on their test papers. These can be stuck
 into their sketchbooks as a colour mixing
 reference and they could annotate them 'red
 and blue makes purple.

※ Remind the children how to dip their brush in
 the water and stroke the brush on the side of
 the pot to remove excess water.
※ Demonstrate how they can make different
 purples not just by using different reds and
 blues, but also by using different proportions
 of red and blue. Show them how to make a
 violet-purple by using more brilliant blue than
 crimson, and a mauve-purple by using more
 crimson than brilliant blue. Paint patches of
 different purples onto A3 paper and tape the
 paper to the board so they can see.
※ Now, working on their cartridge paper, they
 can use a very watered-down, pale purple
 to paint a circle for the flower centre, then
 deeper purples for the petals. They could
 fill in the petals with different depths of the
 same purple by using more or less water.
 They could use more than one purple in each
 flower or different purples for different blooms.
※ Detail in the centre of the flowers could be
 added later in paint or oil pastels in a slightly
 different purple.
※ The stalks and leaves could be added using
 oil pastels or by mixing and painting in
 different greens.
※ When the flowers are dry, they can be cut
 out, laminated and displayed.

Using the work of Hundertwasser (wax relief)

USING SKILL

Time
2 hours

Resources
Newspaper for tables

Per group of children:
Pots of made-up 'Brusho®' in a selection of bright colours
2 or 3 boxes of oil pastels
2 or 3 pots of water

For each child:
A3 cartridge paper
Sketchbook or paper
1B pencil
1 medium long-handled brush

For the teacher:
Access to the work of Hundertwasser:
His drawings of, or photographs of, KunstHausWien houses or other houses he designed, and/or his paintings (eg 'Yellow Houses', 'Window Right' or similar)

National Curriculum
1a,c, 2a,b,c, 4a, 5a

Archie Muirhead, Year 3

Introduction

The Austrian architect and painter Hundertwasser hated straight lines. He felt that straight lines were hard and ugly, so he rounded all the edges on his buildings. He designed buildings to blend in with the landscape, and he liked them to look flowing and natural, as if they had grown out of the ground. You are going to draw (whatever buildings you will be drawing) in your sketchbook, and then you will draw them again in oil pastels as if they had been designed by Hundertwasser. You will then paint over the lines with powdered watercolours. The oil pastel will still show through as the oil in the pastels resists the paint. This technique is called 'wax resist'. You will be using clear, bright colours, just as Hundertwasser did. He loved bright colours, as you can see from his paintings.

Practical activity

※ Show the children pictures of Hundertwasser's buildings and designs and drawings.
※ Ask them what they think of his work.
※ Children should now go outside and draw whatever buildings have been chosen – the school itself would be a good subject.

※ When they have finished and come back inside, ask them to draw the building again in their sketchbooks, as if it had been drawn by Hundertwasser.
※ Remind them that he hated straight lines, and draw their attention to details of roof shapes and windows and the way he drew many lines inside and around his shapes.
※ They could try several different versions of their building.
※ Ask the children to choose what they think is their most successful drawing.
※ Now draw their attention to Hundertwasser's use of colour.
※ Next, the children should select some oil pastel colours and draw their chosen building onto their A3 paper.
※ Lastly, they should paint in all the spaces with bright clear colours of Brusho®.
※ Remind them to wash their brushes between colours.
※ They can go over the lines if they want to, as the oil pastels will resist the Brusho® and it will still show through.

Other techniques and media

Alannah Stenning, Year 3

Other methods of applying paint

It is important to point out that brushes are not the only method of applying paint to a surface. Most children enjoy inventing and making their own painting implements. An example of this is in a lesson on page 88 in the History of painting section. Children should have the opportunity to experiment with such things as fingers, rags, strips of card, rollers and sponges.

Sponges, for example, offer endless opportunities for painting experiments. Rough textures and special effects can be achieved when paints of different consistencies are applied with natural or synthetic sponges of various degrees of coarseness.

Cotton buds are useful as they are easy to hold and are absorbent, and they keep their shape well. They are especially useful for painting small, precise areas, such as petals and stamens of flowers, or for painting in the style of the Pointillists or Aborigine dot pictures.

Fur fabric can be used to apply paint, for example to create a grassy effect.

Single prints can be made from paintings while the paint is still wet by placing a sheet of paper on the top of the painting and peeling it off.

Marbles can be rolled in paint and then rolled across the paper.

Paint can also be:
* Dropped or dripped onto the paper
* Thrown on as in action painting (if you are very brave, have a large space to work in and are prepared for the ensuing mess)
* Splattered on by pulling back the bristle of a stiff brush such as a toothbrush or a washing-up brush
* Sprayed on with a diffuser or an aerosol can
* Blown in different directions along the page through a straw (thin paint or ink)
* Sprinkled onto a wet surface as dry powder
* Scraped with a variety of implements.

Texture

Fabric can be pressed into wet paint to create a texture in a painting.

Thick paint can be applied with a plastic or palette knife to create a rough, uneven texture which is called 'impasto'.

Substances can be added to paint to make it thicker or textured, including PVA, sawdust, salt, starch, flour, icing sugar, crushed eggshells, sand or Polyfilla®.

Paint applied thickly can be scraped with twigs or the ends of brushes to make lines and marks in the paint.

Bits and pieces can be dropped onto thick wet paint such as dry grass, sand, sawdust, tissue paper, foil, thin fabric, netting or glitter.

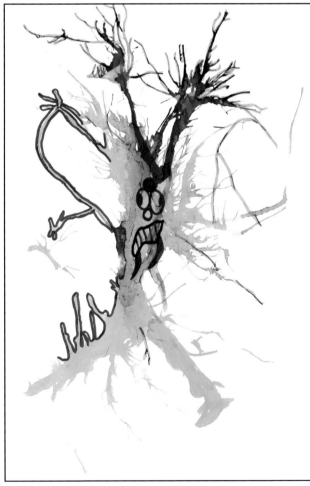

Jordan Wild, Year 4 (blown ink technique)

Blow paintings

SKILL

Time
1 hour

Resources
Newspaper to cover tables

Per pair of children:
Black Brusho® in a pot

For each child:
A4 white paper
A plastic straw
1 medium paintbrush
Protective clothing

For the teacher:
Paper and a straw to demonstrate

National Curriculum
2a,b, 4a, 5a

Year 4 pupil

Note
If children blow too hard and for too long at a time, they may fool dizzy.

Introduction
You are going to try creating some trees, plants and creatures by blowing thin paint along the paper with a straw. You cannot ever be quite sure which way the paint will go, so the end results might not be what you planned. You have to make the best of what happens!

Practical activity
❋ Demonstrate the technique to children by showing the children how to:
  1. Pour a little Brusho® onto the paper.
  2. Place the straw directly above the Brusho®.
  3. Blow very hard down on it.
  4. Chase the paint outwards to make spiky lines.
❋ Explain that they can drop a little more Brusho® on if they want to and continue blowing.
❋ Tell the children to have a go at this.
❋ Explain that they can also crouch down level with the paper and blow horizontally along the surface.

❋ Also tell them that they can chase one Brusho® droplet along in any direction, and if they blow from above, the colour will spread outwards.
❋ Remind them that the Brusho® seems to have a mind of its own.
❋ To make the tree, the children should:
  1. Paint the trunk first.
  2. Add extra Brusho® at the top of the trunk.
  3. Blow the Brusho® upwards and outwards, adding extra black if they need to.
❋ This activity looks beautiful when done in more than one colour, and it lends itself to creating fantasy creatures. Features, limbs, hair, etc can be added later with a fine pen.

Potential pitfall
Children must not suck instead of blow. This might seem obvious, but someone in the class is bound to do it. If Indian ink is being used (not advised), it could be toxic, so check the label.

Spatter technique: making a picture with spattered papers

Thomas Ellis, Year 3 (lifeboat at sea)

Time
2 hours

Links
People who help us/Science/Water

Resources
Newspaper to cover tables
Some old washing-up brushes, nail brushes or toothbrushes
A few old combs
Paper plates for the paints
Coloured felt tips

Per small group of children:
Ready-mixed colours: brilliant and cyan blue, white and green

For each child:
Sketchbook or paper
1 fine-line black pen
2 or 3 sheets of any A4 paper
A4 piece of grey sugar paper
Protective clothing (including goggles if you want to play safe)

For the teacher:
Paper to demonstrate spatter technique
For this picture, access to information and pictures of lifeboats

National Curriculum
2a, 4a,c, 5a

Note

You will need another activity for the rest of the class while a few at a time are spattering paint, unless you have an adult to assist. They could be researching about the Lifeboat Association and drawing lifeboats in their sketchbooks. You also might want to try out the spatter technique, following steps 1–3, before demonstrating.

Introduction

Paint can be applied to a surface in lots of different ways, not just with a brush. You can dribble it, roller it, splat it, print it, sponge it, even throw it onto the paper. Each way creates a different effect. Today you are going to spatter the paint, and when the paint is dry you will be cutting it up and sticking it on paper to create a rough sea picture. Then you can stick on a drawing of a ship riding the waves.

Practical activity

❋ Demonstrate how to spatter paint:
1. Dip a tooth/nail/washing-up brush in one of the paints and hold the brush over the paper (try not to drip on the paper – this is difficult).
2. Pull the bristles back towards yourself and, using an old comb or your fingers, aim the bristles at the paper and release them.
3. As you release the bristles, the paint should splatter all over the paper and probably yourself as well if you have pointed the bristles in the wrong way.

❋ Ask the children to spatter a piece of paper in just one colour, and then experiment with two colours, eg two shades of blue.

❋ They each need to do two or three sheets in different sea colours; white on dark blue and green looks good.

❋ While some children are taking turns, the others could be researching lifeboats, drawing them in their sketchbooks and then drawing one on paper.

❋ This can be coloured with felt tips in the correct lifeboat colours.

❋ When the spatter papers are all dry, the children should cut out wave shapes from different-coloured sheets and stick them onto their grey backgrounds. The lifeboat can be stuck down riding the waves or dwarfed by a giant wave.

❋ The whole picture could be over-spattered with white to represent sea spray.

Creating a batik effect

SKILL

Time
45 min

Links
History/Romans/Greeks

Resources
Newspapers for the tables

For a group of three or four children:
Black Brusho®, mixed in a pot, with
three or four brushes in each pot or
Selection of metallic crayons

For each child:
1 piece of A4 thin white paper

For the teacher:
Some batik fabric
An old iron and a pile of newspaper or
paper towels
Access to pictures of Roman, Celtic,
Viking or Greek metal goblets

National Curriculum
2a, 4a,c, 5a

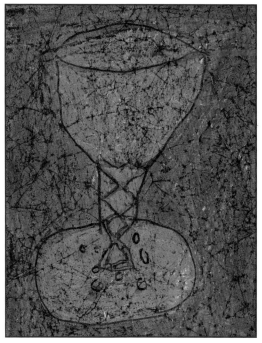

Emma Parkhouse, Year 3

Introduction

There is a technique of printing on fabric called 'batik'. To do batik you need hot wax and special tools, but today you are going to create a similar look to batik but just using crayons and Brusho®. Batik works by painting hot wax onto cloth and then dyeing the cloth with a colour. Where the wax is, the dye won't take. If the wax has been cracked by crumpling the fabric, the colour will get in the cracks and it makes an interesting effect. It is that effect that we are going to try today.

Practical activity

✳ Show the children the fabric and point out the places where the cracks are. If the fabric has several colours, explain that the fabric will have been re-painted with wax and new colours added several times to get a multicoloured effect.

✳ First they should draw their goblets on the paper in pencil, and then colour them thickly in gold, silver, copper or whatever metal they wish them to be (see 'Potential pitfall' below).

✳ Next they should colour the background thickly, in a contrasting metallic colour.

✳ Now tell the children to screw up their drawings. They seem to love doing this, especially if you say, 'What a load of old rubbish, this is going in the bin' and screw

up your own paper. It is a hoary old joke, but they always seem to like it!

✳ When they have screwed up their papers, tell them to straighten them very carefully and smooth them out. You can say 'Nah, I've changed my mind – we'll keep them.'

✳ Then tell them to screw them up again, saying they will be dumped after all.

✳ Then seem to change your mind again and tell them to straighten them again. Warn them that the paper may have become fragile and they need to open them out very carefully or the paper will rip.

✳ The crumpling up and smoothing out should be repeated about three or four times, until the wax crayon colouring is creased and cracked all over.

✳ Now the children should paint over their smoothed paper with black Brusho®. They should paint over once quickly and not do more than one coat, or the colours may go dark and start to disappear.

✳ Finally, when the papers are dry, place each one between two layers of newspapers or paper towels and iron them until they are smooth.

Potential pitfall

In order for the cracked effect to work well, children will need to colour very strongly so that there is a good layer of crayon on every part of the paper.

Line and wash

SKILL

Time
45 min

Links
History

Resources
Newspaper to cover tables

Per pair of children:
Pot of black Brusho®
Pot of water

For each child:
Pen with nib
A5 cartridge paper
Sketchbook or paper
1 fine-line black pen
1 medium watercolour brush

For the teacher:
Access to some pen drawings by Van Gogh

National Curriculum
1a,c, 2a,b, 4a, 5a

Bethany Peacock, Year 3 (the witch's house)

Note
This technique works in a similar way with charcoal and water.

Introduction
Line and wash is a drawing and painting technique that is quite old. Ink has been used in many parts of the world for well over 2,000 years. The ancient Egyptians, Greeks, and Romans used pens made from reeds. The Romans also made pens out of bronze, some of which had nibs shaped very much like the ones we use today. Feather quills were used in Europe in the seventh century and they remained the most popular form of nib until the steel nib was invented in America in the 19th century. The Italian word for feather is 'penna'. The penknife is called a penknife because it was a small pocket knife that was used to cut off the end of a feather to make a pen. You are going to try out using pens with nibs, and then adding a thin wash of ink over the drawings to create tones.

Practical activity
❋ Show the children the pen drawings by Van Gogh and draw their attention to all the different marks he made with his pen.

❋ The children should go outside and draw trees, buildings or whatever catches their eye, in their sketchbooks with fine-line black pens.

❋ Now ask the children to experiment with making lines and marks in their sketchbooks with the pens dipped in black ink. There will be a lot of blots, so they will have to practise stroking the nib on the side of the pot to remove excess ink and transferring the pen to the paper carefully.

❋ When they have gained some control (it is very difficult) over the pen and ink, they should draw some trees on their cartridge paper.

❋ They could redraw items from their sketchbooks or anything they like. Remind them not to be too ambitious, as the nibs are a bit tricky to get used to.

❋ Lastly, the children should dip their brushes in the water and float the water gently over the parts of the drawing they would like to have a little tone. The ink should move a little and a soft, pale grey wash should be created.

Assessment

Year 4 pupil (in the style of Paul Klee)

Assessment of painting

I am tempted to start this section with the subtitle 'If you really must'!

However, if you must, for whatever reason, here are a few pointers.

* You could keep one good example of some work at the end of a unit (say, colour mixing) and put it in a child's record of achievement with comments by both you and the child.
* You could make a note of aspects of painting where a child has excelled or struggled.
* You could make a note about attitude and confidence in relation to painting.
* You could set each child some simple targets at the end of the first term, for example:
  * Work more independently
  * Use the space on the paper better
  * Mix more of your own colours
  * Don't rush to finish
  * Stop now and then and have a think how things are going
  * Don't give up too easily
  * Use less watery paint (ie mix it up more thickly)
  * Remember to use a brush that is right for the job.

The children could add a target of their own and you could check the targets periodically to see if any of them have been met.

* You could photocopy the 'Experience and progression of skills' list for the appropriate year group, from page 9, and highlight in green the ones the children have covered or achieved and in red the ones they have struggled with. That would give you an idea of their weaknesses and strengths, and also what aspects you have covered and what they will need to do before the end of the year or in their next class.
* You could do this for the whole class or make three copies: one for each of a higher, middle and lower ability group. Or, if you are feeling very keen, you could do one for each child.
* These might be helpful when you come to write reports or on parents' evenings when you can't even think what the child looks like, let alone what they can or can't do in painting!

* You can always use lovely phrases like 'Seems to really enjoy painting' or 'Is beginning to develop an understanding of colour mixing'.
* Both phrases, of course mean nothing, but they sound positive and they don't pin you down. So, when the parent says, 'Actually he hates art,' you can reply, 'Well, perhaps that's because I'm such an old crab. But he seems to enjoy actually doing it!' Alternatively, if they say, 'She knows diddlysquat about painting,' you can reply, 'I only said she was beginning to develop an understanding … '

If the bird of Ofsted is due to land on your roof, don't worry. If you have used a range of painting media in different scales and genres, you will have done well and they will be happy. Just make sure that you display a few examples in a prominent place. Remember, if they can't find evidence of it, they may assume it is not happening. If the children have 'done well' then show it off!

Tabitha Waldron, Year 4 (illuminated letter W)

Pupils' self-assessment

You should encourage self-assessment. This should really be happening during the lessons on a regular basis so that the children start to do it for themselves as they are working, without any prompting from you.

Suggest that the children look at their own work and think:
* Am I pleased with it? Why?
* Which bits work the best? Why?
* Which bits don't work so well? Why?
* What would I change if I did it again/worked on it later?
* If someone else had done this, what would I think?
* Have I used the space well?
* What is good about the colours I have used? What is not so good?
* What did I learn while I was doing this?
* Have I made the best use of the paints?
* Does my painting have a particular mood/feeling to it?
* How does it look from a distance?
* Have I done what I was asked, eg shown distance by the use of colour?

Allow time for reflection at the end of a session (if that is possible with the mountains of dirty palettes in teetering piles on the draining board). Children could be asked if they have any comments to make on what they have done, or what others have done. If they are commenting on the work of their peers, encourage a climate of 'being a critical friend' so that their comments are kindly and constructive. You could start the ball rolling by asking one child to select a painting done by another child, hold it up (if it is not dripping wet) and say if they like it and why they think it is good. Then invite that child to choose the work of someone else to comment on. This will give you opportunities to bring out teaching points and reinforce the skills covered in that session.

Connie Ayres, Year 4

Bibliography

Allen, Janet. *Exciting Things to Do with Colour*. Marks & Spencer Ltd

Barnes, Rob. *Art & Design and Topic Work*. Routledge

Clement, Robert and Page, Shirley. *Investigating and Making in Art*. Oliver Boyd

Cummings, Robert. *Just Imagine. Ideas in Painting*. Kestrel Books (Penguin)

Cummings, Robert. *Just Look. A Book about Paintings*. Viking (Penguin)

Fitzsimmons, Su. *Start with Art*. Stanley Thornes

Gombrich, E.H. *The Story of Art*. Phaidon Press

Hart, Tony. *Small Hands Big Ideas*. Guild Publishing, London

Hay, Penny. *Introducing Painting*. NES Arnold

Hayes, Colin. *The Complete Guide to Painting and Drawing, Techniques and Materials*. Phaidon.

Heslewood, Juliet. *The History of Western Painting*. Belitha Press.

King, Penny and Roundhill, Claire. *Portraits. Artists' Workshop*. A&C Black

King, Penny and Roundhill, Claire. *Animals. Artists' Workshop*. A&C Black

Kluge, Gisela. *Drawing, Painting, Printing*. Lutterworth Press

Meager, Nigel and Ashfield, Julie. *Teaching Art at Key Stage 2*. N.S.E.A.D.

Meager, Nigel. *Teaching Art at Key Stage 1*. N.S.E.A.D.

Pluckrose, Henry. *Paints*. Franklin Watts

Pluckrose, Henry. *The Art & Craft Book*. Evans Brothers Ltd, London

Powell, Gillian. *Painting and Sculpture*. Wayland

Richardson, Wendy and Jack. *Cities through the Eyes of Artists*. Heinemann

Solga, Kim. *Paint*! F&W Publications

Stocks, Sue. *Painting*. Wayland

Walters, Elizabeth and Harris, Anne. *Painting: A Young Artist's Guide*. Dorling Kindersley

Wenham, Martin. *Understanding Art: A Guide for Teachers*. Paul Chapman Publishing

Withey, David, Grosz, Jane and Fulton, Maggie. *Art: A Primary Teacher's Handbook*. Folens

Karen Facey, Year 3 (mixing greens)

Glossary

Abstract art
Pictures or sculptures which create an effect using line, tone, form, shape or colour but do not represent anything recognizable.

Acrylic paint
A water-based paint with a plastic binder.

Background
Anything which is behind the main image or which serves as a setting for an image. It can also mean the surface on which a painting is created.

Block paint
Paint that comes in compacted tablets, water-based and generally in basic bright colours.

Brusho®
Powdered watercolour paint that can be made up into a liquid.

Charcoal
Drawing stick made from charred wood.

Chiaroscuro
Italian for light/dark, meaning the use of light and shade in a painting.

Classical
Usually art that is either Greek or Roman or influenced by those styles.

Collage
A French term for describing artwork which includes many items stuck onto a surface.

Complementary colours
Pairs of colours that are opposite on the colour wheel and contrast strongly: blue/orange, yellow/purple, red/green.

Composition
The arrangement of colour, shape, line and so on in a picture.

Contrast
To stand out against something else.

Cubism
A movement in painting that abandoned traditional methods of modelling and perspective and portrayed a subject from several viewpoints at the same time and in simplified planes and shapes.

Elements (of art)
Line, tone, texture. colour, form, shape and composition.

Earth colours
Pigments made from minerals such as ochre, sienna and umber – usually a mixture of browns, greens, blacks and greys.

Egg tempera
Paint using egg as the binder – usually the yolk, but sometimes the whole egg.

Expressionism
A style of art which exaggerates or distorts shape, line and colour to portray feelings.

Fauvism
Painting that uses colour to express emotion rather than reality. The Fauvists worked in the early 20th century to free painting from pictorial representation. Fauves means wild animals.

Ferrule
The metal holder of a brush, where the hair joins the handle.

Figurative
Art that depicts recognizable people, animals or objects; the opposite of abstract art.

Filbert
A conical-shaped brush.

Folk art
Decoration or objects made by people without formal training, who use traditional techniques, patterns, colours and forms.

Foreground
The lower area of a picture, or part of a scene which seems nearer to the viewer.

Thomas Borras, Year 4

113

Form
A 3-D shape, or its representation in 2-D.

Fresco
A method of painting on a plaster wall while the plaster is still wet. The painting becomes part of the wall.

Futurism
Italian movement at its height from 1909–1914, which attempted to capture the beauty of speed and the machine.

Glaze
A thin layer of transparent or translucent paint applied over a picture to create subtle effects. Acrylic paint can be used in this way.

Gouache
A watercolour paint with white pigment added, making the colours more opaque.

Graffito
A method in which a line is produced by scratching through one painted surface to reveal another.

Ground
A substance applied to a support (canvas, board, paper) before the painting begins.

Hue (tint)
A colour or variety of a colour created by adding another colour.

Year 4 pupil

Impasto
The thick application of paint.

Impressionism
A style of painting begun by a group of French artists at the end of the 19th century. They used bright colours, applied freely, to capture the effects of light.

Indian ink
A dense, black ink made from carbon.

Landscape
1. A scene which generally includes some of these elements: fields, hills, trees, grass, rivers, lakes, animals, skies, clouds and rural buildings.
2. In terms of paper or canvas, when the vertical sides are shorter than the horizontal sides.

Lapis lazuli
A blue stone from which the natural ultramarine pigment was once ground.

Media (medium, singular)
In painting, the material the artist uses to make the work of art. A set of materials.

Monochrome
Painted in one colour.

Mono print
A single print taken from a wet image, usually because only one 'take' is possible.

Mural
Painting on walls – implies on a large scale to fill the wall.

Ochre
Natural colours found in different types of earths used to make pigments.

Op art
Developed in the 1960s, paintings that used colour and pattern to create optical illusions.

Palette
1. Slab for mixing colours; can be plastic, china, wood, hardboard or paper.
2. A range of colours at an artist's disposal.

Patron
Someone who supports the arts by commissioning artists to work for him or her.

Perspective
A method of creating a sense of space and distance in a picture.

Pigment
Coloured material which gives the paint its colour, usually ground to a fine powder and mixed with a binder which holds it together and makes it stick to the support (paper, canvas, etc).

Pointillism
A painting technique using separate small dots which merge in the eye when viewed from a distance.

Polyptych
An altarpiece which is made up of several panels that are hinged and can close together.

Pop art
An art movement that was at its peak in the 1960s. The artists took images from the consumer society and popular culture such as television, packaging and advertising. They also used commercial methods of production such as printing.

Poster paint
Water-based, slightly opaque paint, similar to gouache.

Realism
The name given to paintings that try to show the world exactly as it is, even if that means painting unpleasant things.

Sable
An animal whose hair is used for fine soft brushes.

Scumble
To apply a thin, often broken layer of paint over a darker paint.

Sfumato
An Italian word meaning the gradual merging of colours with no sudden changes.

Shade
A colour, especially with regard to its depth or having been made darker by adding black.

Still life
A group of objects arranged together so that they can be drawn or painted. At one time, the objects depicted often had a deep significance.

Stipple
Brush marks made by using the vertical end of the brush, usually consisting of flattened dots.

Surrealism
An art movement which stressed the importance of the irrational and the subconscious. Surrealist paintings usually look strange or disturbing.

Technique
The process or practice that is used to obtain a particular effect.

Tempera
A paint that was originally made up from water, egg and colour. Chemical versions of it are still used.

Texture
Representation in a work of different surfaces, or actual variation in surface caused by the application of thick paint.

Tint
A change in a colour when a small amount of a different colour is added.

Tone
The lightness or darkness of a colour. Also used to describe the shades of grey between black and white.

Under-drawing
The drawing beneath a painting.

Under-painting
Layers of paint beneath the top layer of a painting, particularly those which show through glazes or semi-transparent top layers.

Value
In a colour, this means the strength of one colour from its lightest version to its deepest.

Vanishing point
The point or points at which parallel lines appear to meet on the horizon line.

Wash
A thin, diluted coat of paint applied over a broad area of the surface of a painting, often used as a base for painting.

Shane Sexon, Year 4

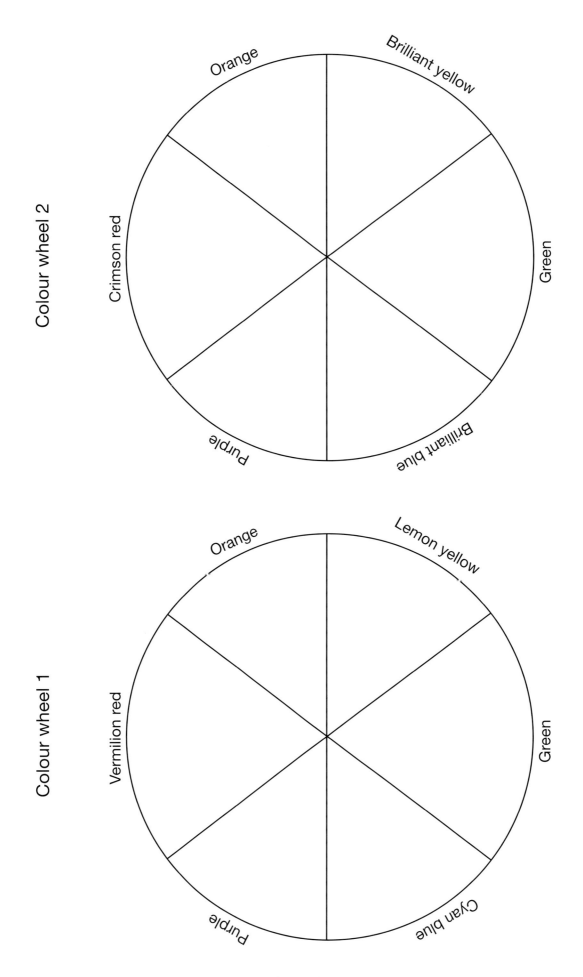

Colour wheel 2

Orange · Brilliant yellow · Green · Brilliant blue · Purple · Crimson red

Colour wheel 1

Orange · Lemon yellow · Green · Cyan blue · Purple · Vermilion red

The colour wheel

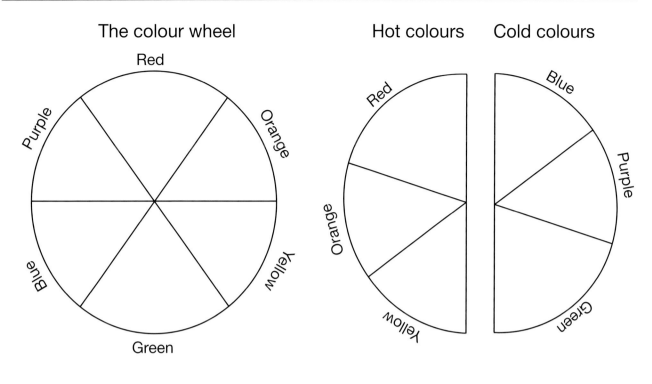

Hot colours   Cold colours

Complementary colours contrast

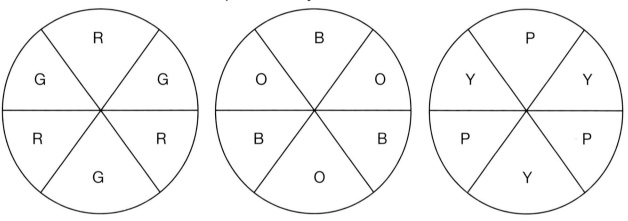

Harmonious colours go well together

Take any two colours that are next to each other on the colour wheel and make three of each.

For example:
3 greens and 3 blues or
3 blues and 3 purples or
3 purples and 3 reds or
3 reds and 3 oranges or
3 oranges and 3 yellows or
3 yellows and 3 greens or …

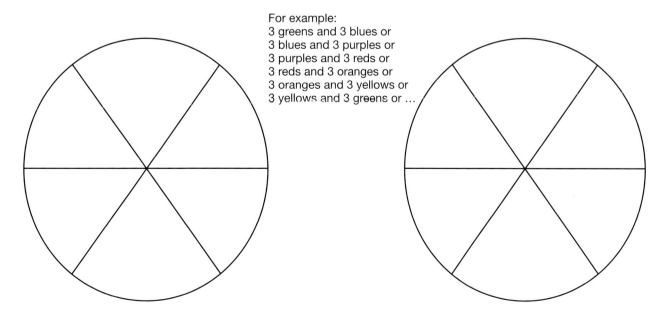

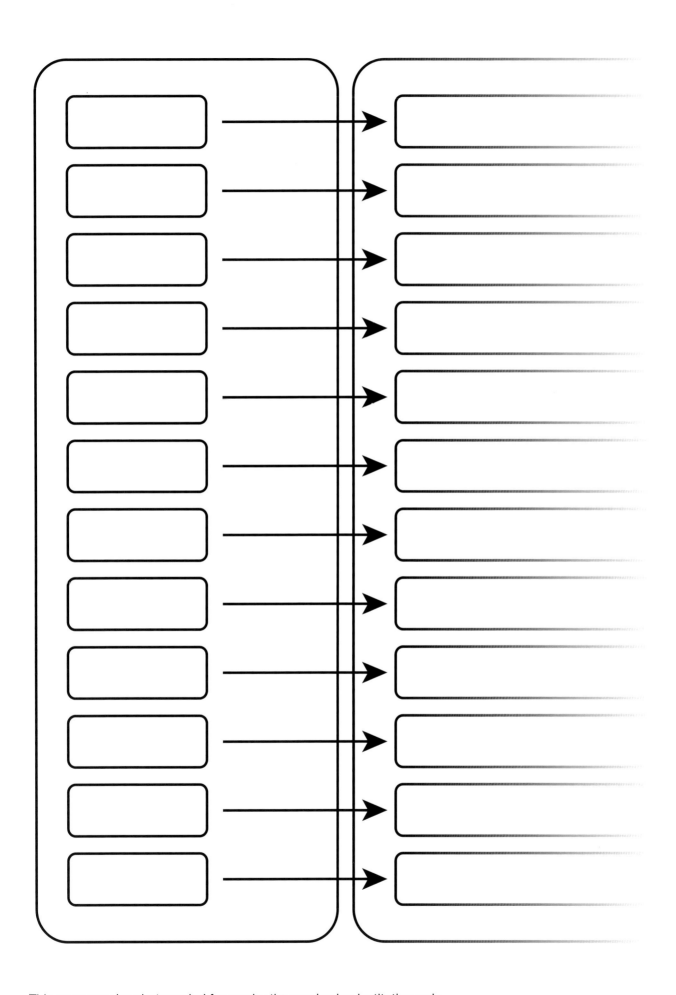

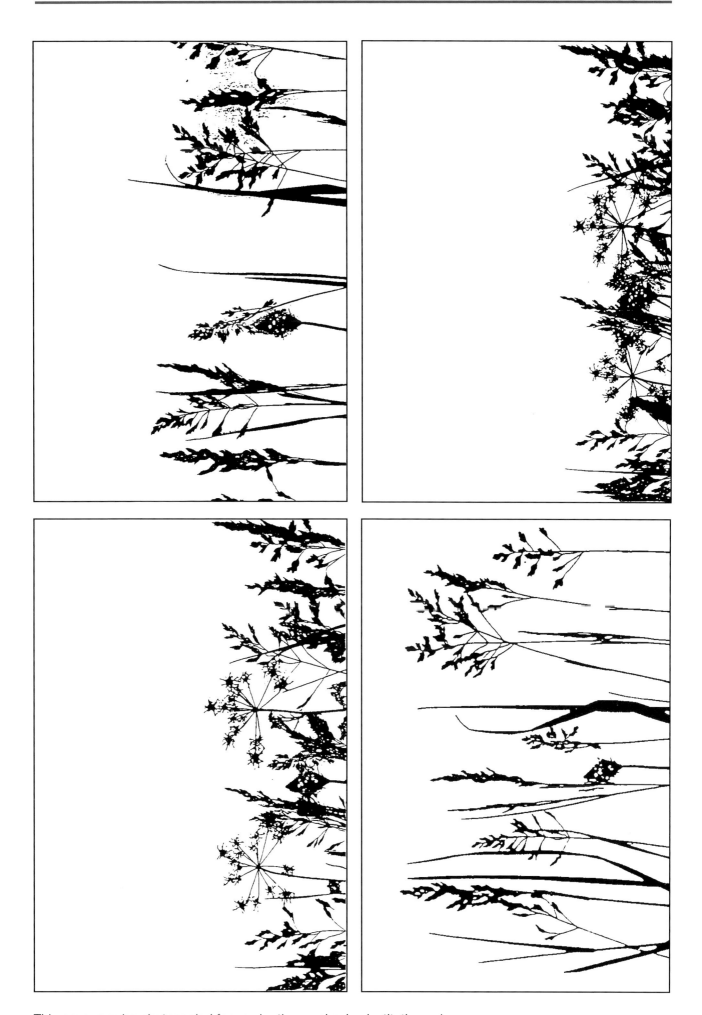

This page may be photocopied for use by the purchasing institution only.